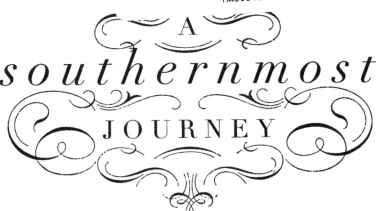

A southernmost JOURNEY

Karen Clark Rasberry

This book is a work of non-fiction. The events and situations are true.

Copyright © 2010 by Karen Clark Rasberry

ISBN: 1453774386 (Paperback)
EAN-13: 9781453774380

All rights reserved. The author gratefully acknowledges permission to re-print columns written for and published by *The ReView of Jones County*, Laurel, Mississippi.

Book design by Erin Rasberry Napier
Contribution by George McNeill
Author photograph by McAlister Creative
Book review by *Mississippi Magazine*
Editing by Cheryl Jones & Phyllis Holder

Printed in the United States of America

Also by Karen Clark Rasberry
The Volley Girls' Book of Life, Love and Unforced Errors
Travelers in Search of Vacancy

For all the kindred souls, past and present,
who have been a part of my southernmost journey.

Because of them, life has been simply, wondrously worthwhile.

CONTENTS

NOWHERE BUT HERE
- 8   The Life Span In Mississippi
- 12 The World Will Never Understand Yoknapatawpha
- 16 It's Not The Heat, It's The Humidity
- 19 The Ten Commandments Of Southern Cooking
- 23 Virtuous Southern Women
- 27 Listen To The Sounds Of Summer
- 30 Singing The Delta Blues
- 33 The Clothesline Standoff

PHILOSOPHICALLY SPEAKING
- 40 A Modern Day Philosopher
- 45 Modern Stock Market Terms
- 49 Bring Back The Board Of Education
- 53 We're Thinking Of A Rainbow Holiday
- 57 Go East, California
- 61 The Folly Of The Blackberry

SOUTHERNMOST JOURNEYS
- 66 Lost In Miami
- 69 The Turnpike And Key Largo Blues
- 72 The Overseas Highway
- 75 In Hemingway's Footprints
- 79 Our Griswald Christmas Vacation
- 83 The Old City Kept Calling
- 87 Rednecks In Paradise
- 91 Sweet On Alabama
- 95 A Very Crude Awakening

ALL PART OF THE JOURNEY

- 102 A Three-Dog Winter
- 106 A Toy Story
- 109 Beau—The Wonder Dog
- 113 Making Peace With The '80s
- 117 Tell Me This Won't Happen To Us
- 121 Once More To The Lake
- 124 The Housedress
- 128 My Life In High Fidelity
- 132 A Card For My Mother
- 136 The Summer Of 1969

MY CIVIL WAR

- 142 All Roads Lead Home
- 146 A Skirmish In My Kitchen
- 149 Springtime At Little Monticello
- 153 The Garden Stage Of Life
- 156 Keep On Keeping
- 159 In Jeep And Bug Love
- 163 We're Gonna Need A Bigger Boat

TO EVERYTHING A SEASON

- 170 The Day Our Innocence Died
- 174 Farewell To The Years Of Aught
- 178 Goodbye To An Old Friend
- 182 A Letter From "Dubya" to Barack
- 186 I Hope You Dance
- 190 Happy Birthday Elvis
- 194 Country Roads Took Him Home
- 198 Salute To A Marine
- 202 A Worthwhile Life
- 206 A House Painted White

nowhere but here

THE LIFE SPAN IN MISSISSIPPI

Mississippi is a wonderfully diverse state with its beautiful forests, charming small towns, the Delta, and what's left of the Coast after Hurricane Katrina. We live life at a little slower pace, open our hearts and doors more readily, worship openly, and give to charitable causes more generously. Despite all the natural beauty and the wonderful characteristics of its people, Mississippi often finds itself on the bottom of desirable lists and at the top of some lists where no state wants to be.

Here is some more disturbing news for those of us who call the Magnolia State home. A recent study of the life spans for men and women in the U.S. showed that we are ranked number 50 at 73.6 years, nosing out Washington, D.C. by a heartbeat, where people can expect to live only 72 years. Hawaii and Minnesota were the states where people can expect to live the longest.

It is easy to understand why people in Hawaii live longer than the rest of us. They are living in a tropical paradise, and they will do whatever it takes to keep breathing. The necessity of dying just so they can go to another paradise probably doesn't seem like such a great proposition.

As for Minnesota, nobody really lives a long time there. It's so cold and the women are so homely, it just seems like it.

Since Mississippi is my birthplace and I plan to be here when I draw my last breath, I was naturally concerned upon discovering that my life span may be shorter than most Americans. At this late date, the extra time gained by moving to Hawaii would be minimal, and I'd probably act like Jack Nicholson in The Shining after one snowbound week in Minnesota, so I will just stay put and be thankful that I don't reside in D.C.

So what makes us die earlier than other Americans? As usual, I stayed up half the night giving thought to this question and came up with the following:

SLEEP DEPRIVATION: Personally, I don't know a woman over fifty who sleeps well at night. We Mississippi belles need more sleep to catch up with Minnesota.

INSECTS: When we were little, mosquitoes used to eat us alive and nobody ever died from it. In hindsight, the main ingredients of the 6-12 repellant my mother slathered all over me must have been six parts sugar and twelve parts blood. However, more bites meant better scratching. In recent years, the West Nile Virus has caused many deaths in our state, which makes me terrified to go into the yard at dusk. Some also think the reason that a lot of Mississippians disappear and are never heard from again is because they are carried off by giant swarms of mosquitoes and drowned in the Bogue Homa and Leaf River swamps. Let us not forget flies, ants and fogs of gnats that have been known to aggravate people to death.

WEATHER: Thanksgiving week is a perfect example of how fickle and potentially lethal the weather is in Mississippi. One day we need wool sweaters and boots and the next it's t-shirts and flip-flops. The human body just wears out its thermostat trying to adjust to the temperature fluctuations. Also, summer in Mississippi drags on for months. The only way to survive summer is to stay indoors with the AC running wide open, which contributes to obesity, suicide, and an occasional homicide. If you go outside, you run the risk of burning alive. Summers here are a danged-if-you-do-danged-if-you-don't proposition. Let me say just three more words about Mississippi weather—humidity, tornadoes, and hurricanes.

FRIED FOOD: Despite repeated warnings from the Surgeon General and our own physicians, Mississippians continue to commit suicide with fried food. If it aint' fried, smothered or covered, we won't touch it. Nothing tastes better than anything fried, but it's clogging our arteries at a rapid pace. No kidding, I witnessed a man have a heart attack just as he finished a meal at an all you can eat buffet. My appetite immediately waned, but the other patrons kept going back for more fried catfish.

LACK OF EXERCISE: Another reason people in Hawaii live longer than we do is because they hula dance, surf, and swim. In Minnesota they do a lot of shivering and trudging through the snow. Mississippians like to live life sitting down, but the lack of movement is turning us into flab. A flabby heart will kill you quicker than the Crescent City bound for New Orleans. Come to think of it, an unnecessary number of us die each year while attempting to cross train tracks.

So, my fellow Mississippians, what are we going to do about this situation? We can't control the weather or exterminate all the insects, but we can park farther away from the all you can eat feed troughs and then perhaps catch a nap on the couch while Fit TV plays in the background. That should add a good three minutes to our lives. Don't take this lightly battered and fried to perfection. In Mississippi, every second counts.

Karen Clark Rasberry

THE WORLD WILL NEVER UNDERSTAND YOKNAPATAWPHA

William Faulkner once said, "To understand the world you must first understand a place like Mississippi." William Faulkner came from an old southern family and grew up in Oxford, Mississippi. Although he only spent a few semesters enrolled at the University of Mississippi before beginning his career as one of the most important writers in the South, the persona of the university and the town are forever intimately entwined with his. To begin to understand Mississippi, the world should visit and explore the place that inspired most of Faulkner's great works.

On our journey to Oxford last weekend for the spring football game, the undulating landscape along Highway 6 on the approach to Oxford was a welcome change from the yellow pollen of the piney woods of Jones County. The stretch of road from Pontotoc to Oxford offers no evidence that up ahead lies the "Harvard of the South." Crooked white houses with peeling paint and derelict general stores dot the highway that leads to the university. It's odd that there are no Ole Miss flags flying or yard signs pledging allegiance to the Rebels. The broken down cars, rusted washing machines and spent possessions strewn about the yards do not indicate that the occupants are either educated or prosperous. It actually appears that the inhabitants have no clue that one of the most beautiful college campuses in the South resides in their backyard. I can't help but wonder how they can live in the shadow of such a great institution of learning and not be affected in some positive way by osmosis or at least revel in the excitement of living a stone's throw from such a storied athletic program. Roadside evidence of a vast societal and cultural gulf is common all over the South, but they glare at you along this stretch of road.

With no prior notice or fanfare, a green highway sign quietly notifies travelers to exit right to the University of Mississippi. It's almost funny how inconspicuous the sign is considering the exit will take you to one of the most respected law schools in the nation, the site of the 2008 presidential debates, a journalism school where many of the great southern writers are in residence, the place where James Meredith paved the way for Civil Rights in higher education and the home of the University Grays who sacrificed everything at the Battle of Gettysburg. It's as if someone is trying to keep the town and the university a secret from the rest of the world.

This is the Mississippi, with all its contradictions, warts and beauty that Faulkner must have been referring to in his quote.

Karen Clark Rasberry

When he was alive, around Oxford they called him "Count No Count" and didn't quite know what to make of him. He loved Mississippi, but Mississippi did not return the love because of his explicit books and liberal views on race until he died in 1962. Around the world, the Nobel Prize winner is called one of America's greatest writers and arguably literary history's most studied author since Shakespeare. His friend, Eudora Welty observed that no man put more of his heart and soul into the written word than William Faulkner. If you want to know all you can about that heart and soul, the fiction where he put it is still right there in Oxford.

Faulkner's fiction begins and ends in Oxford, a place that exposed him to former slaves, old Confederates, alleged ghosts and a cast of memorable characters that only a small town can produce. In his works, Oxford became Jefferson and the county Lafayette became Yoknapatawpha. By transforming real lives and places into fiction, he brought mythological status to the culture of Mississippi.

Faulkner recognized that the world would probably never understand us and would fail to comprehend how important the past is to the present in this state. We natives realize that Mississippi is far from perfect and we are striving to fix what needs fixin'. Our state is the most fertile ground in America for writers, artists, and entrepreneurs. Our history tells the stories of noble fools. It is rich with distinctive people, some who once suffered unspeakable cruelties because of their race. Emotions here run wild and romanticism runs amuck. We have so much hospitality you have to beg us to stop. We are obstinate to a fault about this place we call home. Our state motto could be "Mind your own business. We're doing just fine." It's easy to see why we are often misunderstood and reviled.

I think maybe Mississippi is on the right track with the low-key road signs. Although our reputation for hospitality would forbid it, perhaps we should take it a step further and put up gigantic green signs at every point of entry into the state and all along the borders, saying, "Posted, No Trespassing."

My son-in-law Ben Napier and daughter Erin with Colonel Reb in the Grove at Ole Miss (2010)

IT'S NOT THE HEAT, IT'S THE HUMIDITY

Years ago, a family of foreigners was vacationing at Lake Waukaway while we were there swimming for the day. It was my very first encounter with Yankees. We just couldn't get over the way they talked. They were equally fascinated by the way we expressed ourselves. The language barrier was so vast; we might as well have been from different hemispheres. We said, "I'm on go git a Coke." They said, "I need a pop." We said, "If ya'll don't jump in, you a rotten egg." They said, "Why don't you guys come ohn! Let's go jomp in the watah! A picture of a mob of New Yorkers, shoulder-to-shoulder, trying to beat the heat at Coney Island, provoked this random memory. The scene looked to be less fun than a rained-out picnic. After seeing this mass of humanity standing like cattle in those polluted Atlantic waters,

a southernmost journey

I'll take our oil-tainted Gulf any ole day. Why, Bogue Homa Creek during a dry spell has prettier water. And their so-called beach...I'd rather scrub tar balls off my feet for days than stand ankle-deep in toxic, urban mud.

I don't mean to sound cold-hearted, but it's hard to feel sorry for the residents of the Northeast during this heat wave. They need to come on down below the Mason-Dixon line and spend a July week in Mississippi. They make national headlines for dealing with a few days of 100-plus temps while we have been down here sweltering and swooning since the beginning of time. They say the high temps are much, much worse amidst all that asphalt, concrete and steel. Until those urbanites have experienced a pea patch in July or a hay field in August, they aught not be gnashing their teeth. What about us? We've had hotter Christmases than the lukewarm 4th of July they just experienced.

Summer in Mississippi is about the same temperature as Satan's living room—only more humid. I imagine Hades as having a dry heat while down here in Dixie we get a sticky, steamy situation that makes it next to impossible to draw a deep breath. "It's not the heat; it's the humidity." That should be our state motto—right alongside our state tree—the Magnolia. The air doesn't budge in the summer in Mississippi anywhere—not beneath the pines or in the Delta or on the Coast or in the shade of antique oak trees. The humidity forces it to hover and suffocate every living thing that dares to stick a toe outdoors. If a breeze does stir, it's usually born on the wings of tornadoes and hurricanes.

I'm not complaining, though. It's these languid summers

that are all part of the recipe that makes us who we are. I suspect we all talk so slowly because it takes too much energy to talk swiftly when your brain is about to boil over. In our heads, the words are brisk and coherent, but the heat melts them into sticky decrees before we can spit them out of our mouths. No need to wear yourself out by over-vocalizing. Why say, "I am not going to venture outdoors because it is much too hot today," when you can say, "It's hottern' hell outside."

The unrelenting Mississippi heat has inspired the greatest of the great writers, musicians and actors. Tennessee Williams might never have written *Cat on a Hot Tin Roof* if he had lived in Minnesota. He would have written about cats on ice skates or some silly mess. Elvis couldn't have sung with such soul and passion if he hadn't been born in Tupelo. Instead of being a hunka-hunka *Burning Love*, he could have been a freezing, fluffy pile of snow. And Morgan Freeman most likely wouldn't be one of the greatest actors ever if he had grown up in the Bronx. It's impossible to imagine that voice seasoned with anything but the salt and sweat of Mississippi summers.

They owe it all to the Mississippi heat and humidity. Y'all just think about it and tell me it aint so.

a southernmost journey

THE TEN COMMANDMENTS OF SOUTHERN COOKING

There is a lovely but well-seasoned dining room set that now fittingly occupies the dining room of my husband's first cousin. To a stranger or the un-entitled, the furniture might not appear particularly valuable or ornate. Never mind that one table leg is wobbly from 60 years of Grandpa kicking it with his work boots or that there's a bare spot right in the middle where thousands of skillets of hot cornbread were served.

To those so fortunate to have put their feet under it, feasted, and celebrated being a family, it is priceless. If it could talk, it would tell of many happy times shared over countless meals. It would tell of days filled with more work than leisure, more laughter than tears, more faith than doubt, and more love than anything else.

Although the original owners of that storied dining room set weren't my grandparents by birth, they welcomed me into the fold when I married their grandson. Like my own grandparents and probably yours, too, they were hard working, salt-of-the-earth, sit-down-and-visit-a-spell, genuine folks—the kind that makes the South famous for its hospitality. The simple pleasures of their rural Mississippi life were more than enough to sustain them to an enviable old age.

Over seventy years of marriage proved that Luther and Della Walters were a perfectly mismatched couple. He chose to listen, and she preferred to talk. A World War I veteran, Grandpa was a man who spoke in brief but profound sentences that sometimes only his close family understood. Oftentimes, he would sit solemnly, gazing into the past, perhaps to some distant battlefield, with his striking blue eyes. At other times, he was the contented picture of old age with a tobacco-juice-stained shirt, smiling as if he had just discovered the true meaning of life. On the other hand, Grandma was quite articulate and sociable. Much like a telegraph machine, with her dentures clickity-clacking at lightning speed, she could spread neighborhood news faster than kudzu spreads in May. Some might say that it was gossip, but Heaven knows she would never be found guilty of such mischief.

Without a doubt, one of the greatest pleasures in Grandma's life, besides fishing, was cooking for the ones she loved. She did both with the skill of an artisan. She especially delighted in putting on one of her "weddin' dinners." Let it be understood that a "weddin' dinner" didn't necessarily meant that someone was about to enter the state of wedded bliss. It simply meant that Thanksgiving, Christmas, Easter or a birthday was coming. In Southern terms, there was fixin' to be some serious culinary business conducted in her kitchen.

A "weddin' dinner" at Grandma's house was an all-out attempt on her part to end world hunger and promote a healthy obesity among her descendants. When she cooked, she strictly abided by the Ten Commandments of Southern Cooking. These Commandments weren't actually written down anywhere, but if they were, I imagine they would be found in the Bible of Southern Cooking in the First Chapter of the Book of Martha White:

I. Thou shalt eternally give thanks for the bountiful blessings.
II. Thou shalt have no processed foods before thee.
III. Thou shalt make every single dish with thine own hands.
IV. Thou shalt prepare enough food for an army.
V. Thou shalt put more food on thy plate than thou can eat.
VI. Thou shalt remember the shut-ins and take them a plate.
VII. Thou shalt not use a cookbook or a measuring spoon or a measuring cup.
VIII. Thou shalt serve thy guests, then thyself.
IX. Thou shalt not covet thy brother's pecan pie.
X. Remember that gluttony is a forgivable sin.

Although their season on Earth has passed, Grandma and Grandpa Walters are still very much with the descendents who remain. The uniquely Southern traditions and values they instilled in their children and their children's children live on and bind us together even now.

Grandma left some commandments that are terribly tempting to break as far as Southern cooking goes. This Thanksgiving, if I can just come close to perfecting her cornbread dressing, my family might push away from the table and mimic the now famous words that Grandpa always used after experiencing something wonderful—"That was alright. H'it is, and h'it do."

a southernmost journey

VIRTUOUS SOUTHERN WOMEN

We celebrated my mother-in-law's 87th birthday last Saturday. To commemorate it, we feasted with the extended family on Saturday and joined up again on Sunday morning to give thanks for the life of a virtuous woman. According to Proverbs 31, "A virtuous woman's worth is far above rubies. She does those she loves only good and not evil so she will have no lack of gain. A virtuous woman girds herself with strength. She shall rejoice in time to come. She opens her mouth with wisdom. And her tongue is the law of kindness. She watches over the ways of her household. And does not eat of the bread of idleness. Her children rise up and call her blessed. Charm is deceitful and beauty is vain, but a woman who fears the Lord, she shall be praised."

Ouida Walters Rasberry is a remarkable woman who comes from a long line of Southern women who are tougher than nails, sweeter than molasses, stronger than barbed wire, steadfast as a plow, kind as a saint, and more pleasant than an August evening breeze.

She still powders her nose, pinks her lips, gets her hair curled, and puts a dash of cologne behind her ear before she goes out in public. She looks better when she dresses up for church than most women half her age. Her blue eyes sparkle like morning dew when she talks about her grandchildren. She despises any disarray in her yard and battles it fervently when we aren't looking. One day I had to retrieve her cane from the woods because she accidentally disposed of it along with an armful of fallen limbs. She loves to watch a garden grow, sees God's handy work in every Spring bloom, makes homemade ketchup and cans some of the prettiest ruby red jelly in the South. She does all this despite suffering two strokes and through the sheer determination of a mind that is willing and a body that is no longer able to do many of the things she loves.

She stands less than five feet tall in her Sunday shoes and weighs no more than a sack of potatoes, but she is the mortar that binds our little family together. The thing you have to know is that she is not the only one of her kind. When I married into this family of amazing women over 35 years ago, I never considered that my clumsy feet would someday be called upon to fill their tiny, perpetually moving shoes. So far, I am falling way behind.

The birthday extravaganza was held at the home of my husband's first cousin, Kent Miller, minister of music at West Ellisville Baptist Church. His rambling, turn-of-the-century home is a tutorial in Southern hospitality and charm. Start with a fine antiques emporium, blend in Ripley's Believe It or Not Museum, then add a dash of the Whistle Stop Café and you get a feel for the ambience of cousin Kent's home. It was quite a humbling experience for a woman whose silver and china are all mismatched.

"A virtuous woman also rises while it is yet night." At the age of 83, after working all week at her full-time job with the daily newspaper in town, Aunt Bert Miller was up at midnight and raring to cook the "weddin'" dinner she had planned for her sister's birthday. Weddin' dinners don't have a thing to do with tying the knot, but are more about the family tradition of getting together and widening our girth on the best soul food in the South. It has been my privilege to partake of these dinners for almost 40 years, going back to the days when Grandma Walters was orchestrating them. Believe me, your life is lacking unless you have experienced this cultural and culinary wonder.

Even to the above-average cook, a menu consisting of turkey and dressing, giblet gravy, English peas with new potatoes, cranberry sauce, butterbeans, turnips, sweet potato casserole, sweet tea and homemade rolls would be enough to satisfy the appetite of a field hand. These are mere appetizers for the virtuous Southern cook. To make sure that everyone has to loosen at least one piece of clothing, she throws in pork tenderloin, hot tomato gravy, chicken and rice, hand-cut field corn, snap beans, yellow squash, fresh-fruit salad, hand-shelled field peas, fresh-brewed coffee, birthday cake with inches-thick icing and unsweetened tea for those who are watching their weight.

"Give a virtuous woman the fruit of her hands and let her own works praise her in the gates." Translation: Give a Walters woman a pot and a stove, and she will cook and season with love what she has planted and picked with her own hands and her family will call her wonderful.

Ya'll please pray for me. These are the shoes that I'm called to fill.

Karen Clark Rasberry

Three virtuous Southern women

*The Walters sisters:
Roberta Miller, Ouida Rasberry
& Eleanor Galella (Sept. 2010)*

a southernmost journey

LISTEN TO THE SOUNDS OF SUMMER

Summer is the noisy season when nature comes alive and with the stroke of its brush paints the canvas green and then splashes it with color. It has many different sounds, and if I really listen, bygone summers resonate in my soul. My favorite time to listen is at the end of the day, when the sun melts like orange sherbet into the pine trees in my back yard.

Toward the west, a thicket of trees separates my house from the one where my husband grew up. We bought the red-brick ranch home from his parents in 1980 when our son was three. Five years later, it is where I spent a third trimester soaking my feet in ice water and floating whale-like in the small swimming pool we had built. It is the place where I taught my children and half the neighborhood to swim like tadpoles. The current owners have a young daughter and many visitors this time of the year. My present home has no pool, and the sounds of their frolicking in my old back yard makes me terribly jealous. I hear their giggles and excited screams followed by loud, soaking "ka-splashes." They rewind the tape and play it over and over again. It's not that I hold malice toward them, but those strange children are trespassing on my memories. It has occurred to me that summer belongs to children because they dance so well to its music.

    Like a child's toy accidentally let go into the waves of the ocean, the precious days of summer with my children have floated out of my reach. I can't swim out to retrieve them because the gulf is too big. There's nothing else to do but watch them become smaller and smaller until they are a tiny dot on the horizon. Hearing their joyful summer melody makes me want to repossess my old house and reclaim just one summer day making memories with my young children.

    As summer makes its debut, my back yard has suddenly become a giant aviary filled with all species of birds flitting in and out of the trees. They are happy to be back from wherever it is they fly for the winter. Together they make up a winged chorus that sings one of nature's summer songs. In the distance toward the branch that runs through my neighbor's back pasture, a bullfrog and the Dry Creek choir sings another. As the sun disappears to the west, crickets, cicadas and other nocturnal creatures warm up for their evening serenades. All the sounds of summer cause a lonesomeness to well inside of me. I cannot return to the summers of my prime, but I can visit by walking into my back yard.

    There are so many far-away sounds of summer that are as much a part of me as the heart beating in my chest. Sadly, they are sounds that my ears will never hear again. I will never sit on the broad front porch of my grandparent's old house and hear raindrops galloping on the tin roof...And the way the glass vibrated in the wood-frame windows of my childhood home during a thunderstorm...Or the squeak of the spring and the reverberating sound of the back porch door slamming and my mother's perpetual warning, "Don't slam the screen door! It's going to fall of its hinges one of these days."... Or the promise of a brain-freezing sweetness with the grinding of ice against the sides of a wooden ice cream freezer...Or the roulette table sound of cardboard against the spokes of bicycle wheels...Nor the somnolent whir and about face of an oscillating fan in my bedroom at night...And the mini explosion and clink of the lid upon opening a short bottle of Coke on a box cooler...Never again the juke box songs of the '60s punctuating the fun at Lake Waukaway...No window unit shifting gears in its race against the Mississippi heat...And the rare buzz of a dial tone on the other end of an eight-party line...Or the sound of my own voice calling across the road for my cousins to come ride bikes with me...

The infinite sounds of summer are still out there traveling through time and space. On still summer evenings they ricochet off the stars and return to me in low, humming echoes from the past. Listen to the sounds of summer; and you can hear them too.

My niece Kelsa Temple at our backyard swimming pool in 1983, and her son Isaac Vance now at the same age (2010).

Karen Clark Rasberry

SINGING THE DELTA BLUES

The phrase "having the blues" goes back to 18th Century England, where the "blue devils" was slang for melancholia. But it was sorrows common among blacks after the Civil War, that led to a raw new music—the blues—depicting work, love, poverty, and the hardships freedmen faced in a world barely removed from slavery. Many routes that transverse the South were paved with a people's blues, but no place on Earth is more closely associated with the music than the Mississippi Delta and Highway 61. The broad, rich floodplain—bathed by the Mississippi and washed over and over again by the Yazoo, Tallahatchie, and Big Sunflower Rivers spreads like a great flat blanket 200 miles from Memphis to the kudzu-covered, rolling hills of Vicksburg.

    Until I spent a weekend in Cleveland, Mississippi, at the Senior Mixed Doubles Championship, I never really gave much thought as to why that region gave birth to the blues. Little remains of those post Civil War days but the fertile dirt, the fields and the river—always the river. Although you can't see the river in most of the Delta, you know the muddy water is there, ever churning and twisting down to New Orleans.

The land itself seems to demand the blues. Although we had some respite from the heat after a cool front passed through Friday afternoon, the Delta in summer is normally a place of sullen heat and oppressive humidity where the sun beats down and makes you want to write a blues song of your own. Endless rows of cotton, soybeans and corn offer no relief from the heat or the disorienting flatness of the land. When you stare across the fields from the back seat of a moving vehicle, you tend to lose track of place and distance as one field turns into another and then another until you feel like you are sailing across an ocean of crops. Drowsy towns, like Doddsville, Leland, Merigold, and Mound Bayou that all but died on the vine fifty years ago because of northern migration and the mechanization of crop harvesting, run together like forgettable characters in books. If you've seen one Delta town, you have seen them all. I'm sure the inhabitants there always feel exposed and want to run for cover, into the shady din of a juke joint or into the quiet solace of a church. Both places maybe. Just depends whether it's Saturday night or Sunday morning. After all, the ties that bind the spiritual music of the church and the worldly music of the juke joint are not that far apart—same music, same soul, same key, only the words are different. The lyrics of blues songs are typically about staying, leaving, misery, oppression, the prospect of the hereafter, and better or worse days ahead. Whether they are offered up to God or man, the raw emotion and pleading is always there.

You don't see people working in the fields anymore. The sharecropper shacks, once everywhere, are for the most part gone from the landscape. Every so often you can see one across the distance in the fields, being reclaimed by the land and the elements; and you think many a blues song had to have been sung between its walls.

The thing that brought me to the Delta is also the one thing that most often gives me the blues. I'm very aware that it's a character flaw in me that lets winning or losing at the game of tennis determine my mood. Although my fun-loving team placed 4th in the state, my personal pathetic level of play has inspired me to write a low down, tennis blues song to the tune of B.B. King's *The Thrill is Gone*.

My game is gone...My game is gone away...My game is gone now partner...gone long away... racquet you done me so wrong...and you'll be sorry someday...My serve is gone...it's gone away from me...my volley hit the net too much baby...my game has gone away from me... my overhead went long one too many times now baby...My game is gone away from me...my elbow is gone now too baby...and my back is aching so bad now honey...and now I'm moving oh so slow...how much longer I can stand this pain I don't know...hope my game ain't gone away to stay...game please come back to me...oh, please come back to me and end this low down tennis misery.

a southernmost journey

THE CLOTHESLINE STANDOFF

Here in south Mississippi, we are nearing a drought situation. Right about now it would be wonderful to hear the sound of rain pattering on a tin roof and the way cars sounds like waves crashing when they pass by. If you can name me any sweeter song than the lullaby rain sings on a tin roof, I would like to hear it right this second. This longing for rain has got me to thinking about many of the other simple pleasures that came with growing up as the baby girl of parents whose sensibilities were formed by the Great Depression.

My daddy and mother were born in 1918 and 1923 to parents who were born in the 1890s. They grew up reading by kerosene lanterns and had to sprint to the outhouse when nature called. Of course, television and air-conditioning were luxuries neither of them could even imagine until after World War II. My mother claimed that they made it just fine without all those creature comforts because you don't miss what you've never had.

In 1969, my daddy went to the "Sears and Rareback," as he liked to call it, and purchased a behemoth window unit that completely filled up the bed of the Datsun truck he brought it home in. He had to prop it up with a 2 X 4 to keep it from falling out of the living room window and taking half the house down with it. Window units were jutting out of and propped up in windows all over Jones County, but he currently felt no pressure to stay in step with the changing times. When I whined about how it was so hot and miserable and how I couldn't find a cool spot on the sheets at night, he set me straight. "You don't know hot and miserable until you've spent the night down in the belly of a battleship, scared to death that you are going to be torpedoed by the Japs." Despite the scolding, it was bright and early the next morning that he went to Sears.

Our new air-conditioner had enough BTUs to the cool the Astrodome, if you could just stand the awful roar it made. That thing ran at about the same decibel level as a 747 jet engine on takeoff. He installed it in the living room right next to the television, which made it impossible to be cool and hear the TV at the same time. Since we had to see and hear what was happening on NBC, we only turned it on right before bedtime and opened the doors to the bedrooms. Around 2 A.M., my mother would arise from her sleep to turn it off and open all the windows to save on electricity.

Before we got the window unit, there was the clothesline standoff back in 1967. Mother was perfectly happy with hanging her clothes out to dry on the backyard clothesline. She did agree to get rid of the wringer washing machine shortly after it gobbled up my sister's hand clear to her elbow. To this day, she claims her pinky finger on that hand is a little flatter than the others. I guess that's beside the point. Anyway, Daddy insisted that he wanted her to have an electric clothes dryer. His argument was that she wouldn't have to worry about the clothes getting wet on the line if a cloud came up while she was out of pocket. She was always hesitant to leave the clothes on the line if she had to make a trip into town. In addition it would keep the whole world from seeing an occasional embarrassing pair of holey panties and would keep red wasps out of his boxer shorts. That's another story.

 Her defense was that linens soaked in bleach, washed in Tide, and hung on the line to dry were so much cleaner and fresher smelling. It didn't matter that the towels would dry so scratchy and board stiff that you could lean them up against a wall and they would stand there all by themselves. Sheets weren't much better, but crawling between a fragrant set that had been sun-dried was almost as divine as the sound of rain on a tin roof. If I could only bottle that wonderful scent, I would patent it as Clothesline Sunshine and sell the exclusive rights to Williams-Sonoma. Without a doubt, sensible earthy women from Beverly Hills to Park Avenue would buy enough of it to put me in a beach house on Oahu.

 The standoff finally ended when the aqua blue, Sears delivery truck came creeping up the driveway with a new, Kenmore dryer inside. For years, my mother refused to use it, except on special occasions, because she claimed it took too long to dry the clothes and it kept throwing the switch in the breaker box if the air-conditioner was running at the same time. So much for progress.

Daddy replaced the tin roof with shingles after Hurricane Camille blew through and rolled up the sheets of tin like empty tubes of toothpaste. Come to think of it, I haven't slept well since 1969. When my time comes to depart this life, I hope somebody will haul me to a house with a tin roof, lay me between sheets that smell like sunshine, place a fan at the foot of my bed, and turn a hose on the roof if it's not raining. That way, I will at least be halfway to Heaven. And, if it's summertime, please keep the air-conditioner running wide open.

philosophically speaking

Karen Clark Rasberry

A MODERN DAY PHILOSOPHER

For the past couple of weeks, the Delta blues that I wrote about recently have been following me around like a lost puppy. I moped, groaned and moaned until my husband finally agreed that something had to be done about my back pain. With my doctor's orders secured, I became an inductee into the magical healing powers of S.C.R.M.C.'s Wellness Center. Trust me, if you haven't been a patient there already, it's just a matter of time before some uncooperative muscle, disc, joint, or ligament sends you hobbling through the doors of the old Sears building. Unless my memory fails me, my treatment room was located very near to the former home appliance department where the washers and dryers were once displayed. How appropriate, since I am the queen of washing and drying clothes.

While lying upon a heat pack atop a treatment table with electrodes attached to my lower back area, the electrical stimulation kept sending these weird, random thoughts to my brain. In the twenty minutes that it took to adequately electrocute my taut, painful back muscles into limp strings of spaghetti, the rogue impulses that traveled to my brain practically turned me into a philosopher:

From now on, to preserve my back, I'm only going to bend down to pick up money or jewels.

Even if I knew your social security number, I wouldn't know what to do with it.

If my arms were just a little bit longer, I wouldn't need bifocals.

When I leave the house thinking I look all cute and put together, I never see anybody important. But, if I have to run to the store after a week in bed with the flu and don't wash my hair, put on makeup or pluck my eyebrows, I run into everybody I ever wanted to impress.

I keep some people's phone numbers in my phone just so I know not to answer when they call.

It seems ludicrous that the side effects of some drugs are worse than the symptoms they are intended to cure.

My mother told me to stay out of the sun and now I wonder why my skin looks like a Shar-Pei with age spots.

Karen Clark Rasberry

Sometimes I look down at my watch three times and still don't know what time it is.

Was learning Algebra really necessary?

The only time I look forward to a red light is when I'm trying to finish a text.

How in the heck do you fold a fitted sheet?

Is there such a thing as a total-body lift?

If air travel is so safe, why do airports have "terminals"?

I can't remember the last time I wasn't kind of tired.

Is it just me, or do most airline pilots and doctors look much too wet behind the ears to hold my life in their hands?

I lived quite happily and content for forty years without the Internet or a cell phone; and now I lose my mind if either of them is taken away from me for more than an hour.

I disagree with Kay Jewelers. On any give night, I bet more kisses begin with Chardonnay than Kay.

I have no idea how I gave birth to and raised two children to adulthood and lived to tell about it.

How are you supposed to apply mascara when you can't see your face, much less your eyelashes in the mirror, without your glasses?

I totally take back all those times when my mother forced me to take a nap.

There is a black hole out there somewhere full of lost socks; and I intend to ask God about that when I see him face to face.

Unless you spill something on your jeans, you can wear them indefinitely without washing them.

Putting up a Christmas tree is way more fun than taking it down.

I hate it when I answer my cell phone on the last ring and the caller hangs up. I immediately call back and it rings and rings then goes to voice mail. What's up with that? Did they call to tell me they were dying and croaked before I could call back?

You never see children outside playing these days. Do they ever play chase, red rover, hide-and-seek or hopscotch any more? No wonder there is so much obesity and depression in this country. Children become adults without ever knowing what it was like to be a kid.

Mapquest can skip the first five steps of directions. I'm still perfectly capable of finding my way out of the neighborhood.

Have you ever passed by a full-length mirror in a public place and not recognized yourself?

My back is much better after only a couple of therapy sessions, but with some more electrical stimulation to my brain, I could possibly become a modern day Confucius.

MODERN STOCK MARKET TERMS

Nobody knows, of course, when the stock market will stop its free fall. When the DJIA hit 8000 a few months ago and flirted with 7000 for several weeks, analysts thought that it had surely reached rock bottom, give or take a few points. With the market now making eyes at 6000, the analysts find themselves in the same boat as everyone else in America.... scared and clueless. Today's economy is still no Great Depression—small comfort for those of us who weren't alive in the 1930's but who have heard the stories from our parents and grandparents. With many comparing Obama and his plans to FDR and the New Deal, it's interesting that the market got off to a very bad start in 1933 after Roosevelt was elected, but reversed when he took office (in March) and finished his first year 66% higher. We can only hope that Obama's version of the New Deal doesn't turn into the "Raw Deal" of 2009.

Americans have always been resilient and have prevailed through many trying times in our history. This isn't the first depression, and it certainly won't be the last. Until the economy makes a turnaround, we must remain hopeful, diligent, frugal and try to maintain a sense of humor about the plight we have found ourselves in. In fact, humor might be the key to weathering the rough financial seas that have sent us drifting farther and farther from our own prosperity and dreams of a happy retirement.

My email box is flooded each morning with forwarded emails from my friends, co-workers and family. Some are sentimental and sweet. Others are warnings of impending doom if I drink from plastic bottles or unwashed soft drink cans. Some are hilarious videos gleaned from the best of YouTube. I open most of them, view, chuckle and immediately click delete. However, one timely email I received from my son-in-law this week struck a chord and inspired this column. Unfortunately, I do not know from whence it came and cannot give any individual credit here. Since my brain has been thinking along the same lines, and I have injected more than a few of my own stock market terms, I will lay claim to the authorship.

CEO—Chief Embezzlement Officer

CFO—Corporate Fraud Officer

BULL MARKET—A random upward market movement causing an investor to believe he is a genius.

BEAR MARKET—An indeterminable period of poor performance in the stock market giving investors the reality of retirement when they are deceased.

BROKER—What financial gurus have made me.

STANDARD & POOR—My life in a nutshell.

STOCK ANALYST—Idiots every one. You might as well ask a four-year old which stocks to buy.

MARKET CORRECTION—What happens the day after you buy stocks.

STOCK OPTION—After the market correction, you have no other OPTION but to keep stocks until they go back up.

MARKET SKYROCKET—What happens the day after you transfer every dollar of your 401-K into a fixed interest account.

P/E RATIO—The percentage of investors losing bladder control as the market keeps tanking.

YAHOO—What you do when the stock market is closed for a holiday. You celebrate because you know for certain you won't lose money on those days.

WINDOWS—What my husband will jump out of if the Dow hits 5000.

INSTITUTIONAL INVESTOR—An investor who is now locked up in a nuthouse.

PROFIT—An archaic word no longer in use.

RETIREMENT FUNDS—A mythical sum of money used to fund an imaginary goal.

VACATION HOME—Happy news! You will have two of them—your workplace, and later a small plot in the cemetery.

Here's some food for thought. If you had purchased $1000 of shares of Fannie Mae a year ago, you would have a whopping

$28.00 today. If you had purchased another $1000 in AIG last year, you would have about $7.00 today. If you had purchased $1000 of Lehman Brothers just 365 days ago, you would owe them money today—courtesy of TARP.

Keep in mind that I'm not advocating it but offering this plan in the spirit of good humor. If you had purchased $1000 worth of beer one year ago, (the equivalent of 200 six-packs) drank all the beer, then recycled the aluminum cans, you would have approximately $214.00 and a beer belly. Based on this data, the best current investment plan is to drink heavily and recycle. It's called the 401-KEG.

a southernmost journey

BRING BACK THE BOARD OF EDUCATION

On the first truly cold and frosty morning of fall, I stepped outside to breathe it in. A familiar rumbling of a school bus echoed through the crisp air. The sound of it immediately transported me back to the kitchen window of my childhood home where I would watch for the bus to come lumbering down the road. The bus would sway, rattle and groan all the way to Sandersville School with two kinds of cargo to deliver—those of us who were brushed, shined and hungry to learn—and the ones with sleep in their eyes, tangled hair and not a care that homework was due.

Many miles separate me from the sights, sounds and emotions of my early education. If you have ever returned to your old elementary school, you will find that all the landmarks that once seemed larger than life have been dwarfed by the passage time. Even so, you will most likely recall the little moments that played a gigantic part in who you became.

If elementary school had a color palette, it would have to be the red, white and blue of the American flag to which we daily pledged our allegiance. If it had a fragrance, it would most certainly be the unmistakable schoolhouse potpourri of chalk, crayons, pencil shavings and musty books. If grade school had a flavor, it would definitely not be modern-meat pie, but a tie between lunchroom rolls and the sweet but salty, throat-burning taste of a short Coke filled with snack-machine peanuts.

Somewhere between boarding and de-boarding a bus, hopscotch, red rover, and practicing the Twist on the schoolhouse steps, I learned my ABC's backward and forward, saw Dick and Jane run a million miles, memorized most of the multiplication tables (the 12's eluded me, but the 11's were a piece of cake), and learned not to ever again stick my 4th grade boyfriend, Jerome Harless, in the rump with a needle. Back then, if a girl liked a boy, she sometimes showed it by kicking him in the shins. In my case, it was using him as a voodoo doll. If the feeling were mutual, the boy would let the girl show her affection and never complain. Jerome had evidently enjoyed all the affection he could stand. One sad day, about two weeks into our crush, he tattled to the teacher.

In the sixties, if school had an emotion and a great motivator, it was fear of punishment from "the board of education."

A hush came over the classroom when the teacher called my name and ordered me to the front with her menacing index finger.

It was punishment enough to be placed on public display for my misdeeds; but what came next was worse than the recurring dream I had of being naked in public.

"Do you want me to do it, or shall I send you to the principal's office?" My face was burning hot and red with shame as I nodded toward her wooden ruler. Slap, slap, whap went the ruler across the back of my bare knees. The punishment was over in a matter of seconds. The welts went away; but the lesson learned remained with me for the rest of my school days.

She didn't even have a note from my parents giving her permission to punish me. And, neither did my parents protest or try to have her dismissed. Imagine that.

Forty-five years ago, our biggest fear was being punished with the "board of education." We received essentially benign punishment for basically harmless acts, but it taught us to respect authority. As a result, I didn't wind up in a women's correctional facility, and Jerome became a successful businessman. Then, someone decided that the three P's –punishment, prayer and patriotism were too controversial, offensive and politically incorrect, and should be banished from the classroom.

Flash forward a few decades to Columbine, Pearl High School and Virginia Tech...

For the most part, the problems with education are not the fault of the teachers, curriculum or administrators. It is a societal problem where God, character, ambition, and discipline have been replaced with secularism, misguidance, indifference and disregard for authority.

Great education is a multi-faceted process that cannot be accomplished in a day, a month or even years. I realize that there is no magic potion or pill that can be swallowed to make it all better. But, if we could somehow bring back prayer, the Pledge of Allegiance, and respect for the "board of education," just imagine what might happen in the classroom.

a southernmost journey

WE'RE THINKING OF A RAINBOW HOLIDAY

Many of you probably received an e-mail that was making the rounds a while back. In this e-mail, Ben Stein, a well-known lawyer, actor, commentator and most importantly, a Jew, made some very surprising comments about Christmas. He revealed that it does not bother him when people wish him merry Christmas. He does not feel threatened or discriminated against at the sight of beautiful, bejeweled Christmas trees. Further, he adds that as a Jew, he doesn't like being pushed around because of his ancestry and religious convictions, and that he doesn't think Christians like getting pushed around for being Christians. Mr. Stein thinks that people who believe in God are sick and tired of getting pushed around, period. The question is, what are we going to do about it?

Unless you have been living in a cave somewhere, you know there is an all-out attack on Christmas and attempts by certain interest groups to eradicate the traditions that most of us hold dear to our hearts. They object to public displays of Nativity scenes, Christmas trees, etc., and are elated that some school systems have renamed Christmas break the winter break. They have already forced prayer out of our schools and the Ten Commandments out of courthouses, and they won't rest until they steal Christmas. If we, who are in the quiet majority, continue to sit idly by and allow the very loud minority to dictate how we celebrate the most important event in history, then we shouldn't be surprised one day when we risk imprisonment if we wish the wrong person a merry Christmas.

I fell asleep one night after watching Bill O'Reilly interview an atheist on this topic and was jolted from my sleep when Bing Crosby and Irving Berlin visited me in a dream. They were distraught because their beloved musical masterpiece, *White Christmas*, had been banned from the airways because it was considered too offensive. With over 30 million copies sold since 1942, *White Christmas* is the largest selling Christmas single of all time. Their visit compelled me to objectively dissect each word of the song to analyze how it could possibly be perceived as offensive.

I'm: It's too selfish sounding. It must be changed to we're to include everybody.

Dreaming: Might sadden those who don't get enough REM sleep. Substitute with the word thinking. Of course, use of this word might offend those countless people who don't think. On the other hand, they won't realize they should be offended because they don't think.

Of a: Nothing offensive there.

White: This word definitely has racial undertones. Substitute with rainbow.

Christmas: This is the real point of contention in the song. It makes non-Christians sick to hear it. Substitute with holiday.

Just like: Sounds like slang to me. Substitute with similar to.

The ones: Acceptable.

I used to know: The grammar is too run of the mill. Might be an insult to the highly intelligent. Change to I once experienced.

Where the treetops glisten: Doesn't apply to those who live where there are no trees or snowfall. They might feel left out. Change to where we happened to dwell.

And children listen to hear sleigh bells in the snow: This line might disturb child-haters, the hearing impaired and Floridians. Substitute with and everyone observes merriment in the multi-colored landscape.

I'm dreaming of a white Christmas: Must be changed to we're thinking of a rainbow holiday.

With every Christmas card I write: Hardly anyone pens Christmas cards these days. We send e-greetings because they are free and easy. With each holiday message we send is more in keeping with the times.

May your days be merry and bright: Might be disconcerting to those on death row, the clinically depressed, or people who enjoy being grouchy all the time. Edit to may your existence be comfortable and well lit.

And may all your Christmases be white: And may all your holidays be whatever color you like.

*We're thinking of a rainbow holiday
Similar to the ones we once experienced
Where we happened to dwell.
And everyone observes merriment
In the multi colored landscape.
We're thinking of a rainbow holiday
With each holiday message we send.
May your existence be comfortable and well lit,
And may all your holidays be whatever color you like.*

If I must say so myself, the revised lyrics do have a catchy ring to them. Why, I don't believe Mr. Berlin could have rewritten it better himself. You might want to go ahead and memorize them, because sooner or later you will have no choice unless we do something to stop the madness.

Through this printed medium, please permit me to do my part. MERRY CHRISTMAS!

Erin on Christmas morning (1987).

GO EAST, CALIFORNIA

After the apocalyptic earthquake hit Haiti, I heard a news report predicting that southern California has a 99% chance of being hit with an earthquake of 6.7 magnitude or greater in the next thirty years. Those odds are as great as Mississippi's chances of having a hot and humid summer sometime during the next thirty years. The last major earthquake to hit California was the Northridge quake of 1994. After sixteen years without a major shake, it seems to me that our liberal, west-coast friends are hanging onto the West Coast by a thread. If I lived in California, I think I would move tomorrow.

They say that San Diego has near-perfect weather year round and a agreat zoo. Every morning when I tune into the Weather Channel, I make it a point to check the weather in southern California. Winter, Summer, Spring and Fall, the forecast is practically always for blue skies, low humidity and temps in the '70s. Our beloved state only enjoys those three climatic conditions in unison about three days out of each year—usually in October. We do have more than our fair share of hurricanes and tornadoes here in Mississippi, but at least the earth doesn't move under our feet like an escalator. We do have at least a week's notice when hurricanes are about to strike, and at least a few minutes warning to run from twisters. Pray tell, how can you prepare for the earth to suddenly open up and swallow you whole?

Name me a city more intriguing and beautiful than San Francisco. That fair city where the sun sets has the Golden Gate Bridge, trolley cars, and the bay. Hollywood is the center of the universe as far as moviemaking, entertainment, shopping, and beautiful people. Los Angeles, the City of Angels must be absolutely wonderful or a gozillion people wouldn't be living there. Although I never visited there, people say the Napa Valley is comparable to the Mediterranean with its mild climate, vineyards and breathtaking countryside. Even with all that natural beauty, I would still move tomorrow.

For me, living in such a circumstance would be like waiting for the other shoe to drop. Despite the threat of earthquakes, most Californians say they will never leave because there is nowhere else they want to live. The state is completely broke, illegal immigrants are taking over, and it could fall into the Pacific Ocean at any time. That's fine for them, but I would sell my house and head anywhere but there. Even if I couldn't sell my house, I would hand the keys over to the bank and get the heck out of Dodge.

If I lived in California and had children, that would be another reason to move away. Imagine the nightmares that a small tremor—not to mention a pretty big one— could spawn in children. Some adults can deal with living on a fault in the Earth, but I'm concerned about how many kids can.

There's no question that because I don't live in California, don't have family there, don't earn my living there, it's fairly easy for me to say I'd get out before the earth started shaking like a paint mixer at Sherwin-Williams. Where would I go? Not New York—too much humanity, too expensive and the city lives under the ever-present threat of another terrorist attack. Not Atlanta—too much gnarled traffic and too many obnoxious, transplanted Yankees. Definitely not Memphis. I moved my daughter there for a summer and got robbed within the first ten minutes of our arrival. Never in a million years would I move to Miami—don't speak the language, plus that part of Florida reminds me of an appendix just dangling there waiting to cause trouble.

Let's keep this our little secret from Californians, but if I lived there I think I would move to where I live now—-good ole Jones County, Mississippi or at least somewhere in our fair state. Mississippi is sparsely populated with friendly folks. We aren't overrun with obnoxious northerners. Hopefully, Al Qaeda has bigger fish to blow up than lil' ole Mississippi. The robbers mostly rob each other. I can speak the southern English language with the best of them. The two biggest things we have to worry about are hurricanes and tornadoes. However, we have already lived through the worst of them and have become wiser and better for it. Chances are, another Katrina or Glade tornado won't come along for many, many more years. Even if they do, we will still have the ground left to rebuild on.

Karen Clark Rasberry

After doing some research, I think Californians should flee to Arizona where the climate is wonderful and the threat of natural disasters is little to none. Plus, when the really big one hits California in a few years, they will be sitting pretty on their oceanfront property on the new West Coast.

a southernmost journey

THE FOLLY OF THE BLACKBERRY

The world is just getting too complex for me. Or, maybe I'm just getting too old to keep up with the complexities of the world. Most of my difficulties come via the very gadgets that were intended to make my life much more simple. When I first bought my Blackberry, it was out of peer pressure from the younger folks that surround me. I wanted to feel important and be on the cutting edge with all the young whippersnappers. In hindsight, I realize that I need a Blackberry as much as a moose needs a hat rack. I lived the first half-century of my life without a cell phone that plays music, takes videos, pictures and communicates with all my friends on Facebook and Twitter, and made it just fine. If they could invent a smart phone that can do something really useful, like clean my commodes for me, then that $120.00 per month would be more than worth the price.

Currently, I'm paying hard-earned money for something that has become more of a nuisance than a necessity.

Thanks to my Blackberry e-mail, I can instantly know what perils or blessings await me if I simply answer the call of that little, incessant, red, blinking light. Because of it, I no longer drink Coca-Cola because it can remove toilet stains...I no longer use Cling Wrap in the microwave because it causes seven different types of cancer...I am terrified to open a bathroom door without using a paper towel, or have the waitress put lemon slices in my ice water without worrying about the bacteria on the lemon peel...I can't use the remote control in a hotel room because I can only imagine what the last person was doing while flipping through the adult movie channels...And thanks to my Blackberry, I can't ever pick up a penny dropped in a parking lot because it might have been planted there by a sex molester waiting to grab me as I bend over...I can't do any gardening because I'm afraid I'll get bitten by a violin spider and my hand will fall off...I am also especially grateful to my Blackberry for warning me that rat droppings are in the glue on envelopes...For the same reason, I now have to scrub the top of every drink can before consuming the contents...I now keep my toothbrush in the living room because my smart phone warned me that water splashes over 6 feet out a toilet when you flush it...I now smell like a water buffalo after playing a tennis match because deodorants cause cancer...One bright spot is that I no longer have to worry about my soul because 795,213 angels are looking out for me, and St. Theresa's Novena will grant my every wish. I heeded the warnings and faithfully forwarded each and every e-mail to at least ten people within the allotted ten minutes to insure that a miracle would befall me within the next twenty-four hours. Strange, though, I'm still waiting for those miracles to arrive.

I am worn out with living like this. My Blackberry has now become an addiction—a monkey on my back—always waiting for me to flip it open to get another fix. I can't eat, sleep, sit quietly in church or even write a column unless it is within my view and reach. As pathetic as it is, I haven't even mentioned the folly of predictive text messaging. Without benefit of good eyesight and adequate lighting, some of the messages I've sent are enough to have me committed to the nearest insane asylum.

If you sent a friend who was vacationing in Florida the following text message, what would she think about your mental status? "How's the weapons in sinners florist?" Exactly. I simply wanted to know, "How's the weather in sunny Florida?" Try texting this to a fellow Realtor when you want to show one of their listings..."Hide the jet under the dope hut" in lieu of "hide the key under the door mat." Texting by old, far-sighted people can occasionally lead to marital discord—"Wish you were her." Even an innocent request for your husband to leave the lights on because you will be home soon can lead to a big homecoming surprise—"Will be hot soon. Leave the lust on." A message to my sister while we were both watching a documentary on Thomas Jefferson and his beloved home in Virginia, affirms that I need to trade in my Blackberry for a carrier pigeon. "I want to take another trip through virginity." The hilarious thing is she didn't question my message or skip a beat with her reply. "Me too. That would be wonderful."

southernmost journeys

Karen Clark Rasberry

LOST IN MIAMI

In a fit of the winter doldrums last January, I announced to my husband that I wanted to visit Key West this summer for our 35th anniversary. His response was not the enthusiastic one I had hoped for, "Well, have at it. Who's going with you?" After several months of a Mexican standoff—his weapon being a vow to never fly again, and mine—a vow to never drive over six hundred miles to a Civil War battlefield again (re: Gettysburg), we reached a compromise. We would fly to Miami, rent a car and drive down the Keys to the Conch Republic—to the languorous city of Buffett, Hemingway and Mallory Square.

    The truth is, I used my cunning female wit and charm to bribe him into boarding a lofty death trap again, promising that we would visit any Civil War battlefield of his choosing, that I would chauffer him the entire distance both ways, and that I would stand shoulder to shoulder with him as he slobbered over every cannon, artifact and battlefield map and that I would listen adoringly to his educational monologues of fallen generals and unbelievable human bravery and sacrifice. This offer was subject to one condition: Neither of us could use the phrase "I told you so" if our chosen trips went awry.

Since Phil had not set foot in an airport since before September 11, 2001, he was very heartened by the new airport security measures. He didn't seem to mind the wait, the hostile security persons, or having to spread eagle for a burly man to run a magnetic wand over all his body parts after a pin in his ankle set off alarms.

The flight was uneventful except for an O.J. Simpson-like dash through the Atlanta airport to make the Miami connection that was set to depart 10 minutes after our flight from Jackson touched down. Thanks to tennis and the Stairmaster at the Wellness Center, we made our connection with 30 seconds to spare.

So far, so good, with no real incentives for "I told you so's" yet.

My romantic views of Miami had no basis except for what I had seen in movies and on television. I had envisioned us as Crockett and Tubbs cruising down the glitzy, palm-lined streets of South Beach to the strains of Phil Collin's *In the Air Tonight*. In reality, we were more like Steve Martin and John Candy in the movie *Trains, Planes and Automobiles*, driving in circles in a rented Kia listening to the strains of Cuban music, hopelessly lost in a seemingly foreign country.

The 2008 census shows that Miami had a population if 413,201 people. Of that number, 65.8% are Hispanic and only

11.8% are of the Caucasian persuasion. The city alone has 96 different zip codes. Jones County has less than ten that I always have trouble remembering. My dear friends, that is a few more people than you will see at the Laurel Wal-Mart on Saturday afternoons. For a couple of rednecks that get stressed out over the morning traffic on Lower Myrick Road, just let me say that we feel lucky to still be alive.

The map and directions to the turnpike they gave us at the car rental desk seemed simple enough. Happy Floridays! We would be on U.S. 1 headed to paradise in a matter of minutes. Forty-five minutes later, after leaving the airport behind us and to our right, we found ourselves approaching it again on our left. Perhaps, I was holding the map upside down or they played a cruel joke on us that would purposely add days and miles to the rental car. We pulled over at a curb store. With the map in hand, I pointed and asked how in the world does one from Mississippi get to the turnpike from here? Everyone looked at me warily as if I had just landed from Mars. "No Engleesh," they all said while shaking their heads. Back inside the car, I bleated tearfully, "Are you sure we landed in Miami, Florida in the United States of freaking America! What if we are stuck here forever, left to fend for ourselves in an American city where we don't speak the language? What if they don't use dollars here? We won't even be able to buy gas or food." We were foreigners in a strange land, starving and sleep deprived, with dreams of a perfect second honeymoon fading in the Miami heat like the deodorant I applied at 3:30 A.M. that morning.

Although they were on the tip of his tongue, out of pity for our situation, Phil didn't dare utter those four fighting words yet.

a southernmost journey

THE TURNPIKE AND KEY LARGO BLUES

Last week's column ended in a cliffhanger with Phil and me hopelessly lost in the Cuban ghettos of Miami trying to make our way to the Florida Turnpike. It's very surprising how many of you are just itching to know what happened next. Obviously, we did make it out of Miami or I wouldn't be writing these words from the comfort of my own home.

Have you every heard the old saying, "even a blind sow will stumble up on an acorn every now and then"? It was blind luck, pure and simple, that led us out of Miami onto the turnpike. However, the turnpike was not the portal to paradise we had imagined. It was just another conundrum in a long list of challenges that we didn't foresee.

Acclaimed as the "Less Stressway" for maneuvering up and down the peninsula, the Florida Turnpike has been practicing highway robbery for fifty years. It spans 312 miles from U.S. 1 in Florida City to I-75 in Wildwood. They hold you up when you enter it. They stick it to you when you leave it. They ambush you when you least expect it. It's like a multi-laned prison with the freedoms of the outside world all around you. If you break out for food, gas or restrooms, you know you are going to pay. They do appease you by allowing you to cruise freely at 70 M.P.H. for a few miles. Then, for no good reason, they tighten your shackles with another tollbooth just when you think you've made your great escape. After finally stumbling onto it, eighteen toll booths later, we limped off of it onto U.S. 1 in Florida City. By that point, I was digging in my purse and checking under the seats for quarters to pay the final 50 cents for bail from our highway imprisonment. Although I have compared the Florida Turnpike to a prison, it just occurred to me that there is another very appropriate comparison that could have been used—pay toilets in the Rotavirus wing of a hospital.

With the lost nightmare of Miami behind us, Key West in front of us, the Gulf of Mexico to our right and the Atlantic Ocean to our left, we entered Key Largo at mile marker 106. Key Largo is the first and largest key in a chain that is comprised of hundreds of spits of land that divide the Gulf of Mexico from the Atlantic Ocean.

Softly, I heard the Beach Boys harmonizing in my head "Aruba, Jamaica, ooo I wanna take you, Bermuda, Bahama, come on pretty mama, Key Largo, Montego, baby, why don't we go...." Although Key Largo was once the setting for a movie by the same name in 1948 and is also featured in that catchy song that was one of the catalysts for making our southernmost journey in the first place, that shining jewel in the sea has apparently lost its glimmer.

We could see not a glimpse of bodies in the sand, no falling in love to the rhythm of a steel drum band and certainly no rush of a tropical contact high—only boarded-up souvenir shops, abandoned boat hulls and dilapidated mom and pop motels. After the music faded from my consciousness, and my dream of the perfect getaway was dealt yet another dose of reality, the gloom inside the car became palpable. This sad turn of events was not my fault. I just couldn't believe that the Beach Boys had been lying to me all these years.

As the heartbreaking sight of a once glittering resort turned into a ghost town rolled past the windows of the Kia and with not a drop of turquoise-blue water in sight, I turned to Phil with an embarrassed grin and waited to hear those four little words that I so expected to hear. In keeping with our promise, he substituted four allowable words in an exceptionally "I told you so" tone of voice.

"This ain't exactly paradise."

THE OVERSEAS HIGHWAY

As Phil and I made our way further south out of once glittering Key Largo, a quotation from Ernest Hemingway summed up the situation best, "Never go on trips with someone you don't love." If we did not have love for and mutual understanding of each other and had not shared thirty-five years of marriage, I'm quite sure he would have put me and my pregnant looking suitcases out on the side of the road somewhere around Boggy Key. If I had not born his children, I'm almost positive that he wouldn't even have glanced in the rear view mirror or tapped the brakes in remorse as he pointed the Kia north toward home.

In a nick of time, to save me from hitchhiking alone to Key West, the landscape around us began to change dramatically. Around mile marker 84 at the beginning of a cluster of keys known as Islamorada, the gloomy mood in the car became lighter, buoyed by the sight of charter boats cutting silver streaks through the turquoise-blue water as they returned to shore with the catch of the day. For my husband, if there is one thing more beautiful or moving than a Civil War battlefield, it would have to be the sight of a boat loaded with fish.

The "purple isles" or Islamorada is acclaimed as the "Sport Fishing Capital of the World." Islamorada provides a jumping off point to world-class deep sea and backcountry fishing. Because the Gulf of Mexico and the Atlantic Ocean are married in the Keys, every species of fish in the Northern Hemisphere can be found in the intermingled waters. Although I could see the lust in my husband's eyes and a longing look on his face not witnessed by me since he laid eyes on the "High Water Mark of the Confederacy" at Gettysburg, we could not tarry in that angler's paradise.

Reservations at Henry Flagler's Casa Marina Hotel would not wait. The call to Key West, the same one that had beckoned explorers, pirates, bohemians, creative spirits, and presidents, was still forceful enough to keep my husband from dropping anchor in Islamorada.

The road that now lay ahead of us was the postcard picture that I had imagined last January. Imagine a narrow ribbon of asphalt and concrete suspended between emerald seas and azure blue skies. Add a generous taste of exotic plants and blooms, the country's only coral reefs and a romantic history with tales of buccaneering pirates and buried treasures. Then, dangle it off the southern tip of Florida, and you have the Overseas Highway. It runs along the footprints of

Henry Flagler's East Coast Railroad that once connected his resort hotels in St. Augustine and Palm Beach to Key West. After its completion in 1912, the railroad had cost Flagler fifty million of his own dollars and hundreds of lives. It lasted only two decades before the worst hurricane of the century in 1935 destroyed all the tracks. The state of Florida purchased the remains for $650,000 and proceeded to convert it into a two-lane highway that opened in 1938.

As much as I was disappointed in the ramshackle area around Key Largo and the uglification of some of the other areas we passed through, I was equally mesmerized by the pockets of unspoiled nature along the way and how underdeveloped the area is compared to high-rise infested beaches at Orange Beach and Destin. Bahia Honda State Park was one such area where you can still get a taste of the old Florida I remember from childhood vacations.

Somewhere in the middle of the Seven Mile Bridge at mile marker 45, *Conky Tonkin'*, a song that only true Parrot Heads know and love, came to mind...."Hop inside, I'm headed south, take a ride headed down U.S. 1. Havin' too much fun to turn back, we're explorers in a rented Kia. We are going conky tonkin' trying to catch up with the sun. Do you wanna see the rest, I said I haven't a care, Phil, just take me there, and we drove all the way to Key West..."

With only 44 miles to go and "I told you sos" a world away from our thoughts, the excitement between us was more than enough to propel us all the way to Cuba.

a southernmost journey

IN HEMINGWAY'S FOOTPRINTS

Have you ever had an image of someone or something in your mind that proved to be totally wrong once you met that person or finally laid eyes on the thing you had constructed in your imagination? When we finally reached Key West, it was similar to Ponce de Leon's discovery of Florida while he was searching for the Fountain of Youth. Not what he was looking for, but it didn't turn out half bad. I'm sure we felt like Ernest Hemingway did when he first stopped there on a return trip from Paris. It is a town unlike any other we have ever experienced. It is a moveable stage for a cast of characters that could be straight out of one of Hemingway's books. It offers a little bit of something for everyone—from the seekers of seediness to the respectable family of tourists—it leaves you wondering why you were looking for something else in the first place. From the quaint conch houses hidden behind fences among lush tropical vegetation to the million dollar Victorian cottages draped in bougainvillea to its unique shops and open-air art galleries, it did not disappoint. From the clothing-optional landmarks to the desperately irate taxi driver with a $4,000 a month mortgage to the scraggly character sitting on the corner selling dirty jokes for a dollar to the young waitress who moved there to live with her transvestite uncle/aunt to the hollowed-eyed girl who wanders aimless and barefoot through Mallory Square all day, it is a tropical buffet table of life, literally and figuratively, that offers something for every palate. Key West is a small spit of land only eight miles square anchored in the waters between two great oceans. Even with water everywhere, if you are seeking white, sandy beaches, aquamarine water and waves crashing to shore, you will not find it there. Unknowingly, we went there seeking to taste one thing, but instead, we got a taste of the unexpected and returned home completely satiated by what we got.

  Our hotel was built in 1920 in the grand style of old Florida by Henry Flagler as a sister hotel to the Casa Monica in our beloved city of St. Augustine. It is located on the Atlantic side of the island near the southernmost point in the continental United States and a short walk to several points of interest. With 1100 feet of ocean frontage, Casa Marina has the largest beach, public or private, on the island. Due to the fact that the third largest coral reef in the world encircles the island about seven miles offshore, the water is mostly shallow and laps gently onto the grayish, crushed shell beach like the waters at Bogue Homa Lake. It wasn't the Fiji-inspired vision I had imagined, but hammocks suspended between crossed palm trees and an interesting parade of sunbathers, including a geriatric tycoon wearing a black Speedo and a pinup-worthy babe on his arm, made people watching more interesting than the book I purchased at Hemingway's gift shop.

I would be remiss if I didn't tell you that walking in Hemingway's footsteps was definitely my favorite part of the trip. Hemingway was a man's man who lived a lusty, bohemian lifestyle in 1920's Paris as part of the expatriate artistic and literary world of the Lost Generation after World War I. He kept company with the likes of F. Scott Fitzgerald, John Steinbeck, Cole Porter and his good friend, the artist Waldo Pierce. He left Paris and moved to the island of Key West with his wife Pauline into a house paid for by her wealthy uncle. It was there that two of his three sons were born.

It was in that location in a studio above the garage where he wrote approximately 70% of his life's work. Many of the characters appeared in his book *To Have and Have Not*, including Sloppy Joe Russell, owner of the famous Sloppy Joe's Bar located at the end of Duval Street. When he wasn't fishing in the Dry Tortugas with his pals or drinking with them at Sloppy Joe's, he and his aching head managed to write *Death in the Afternoon* and *The Sun Also Rises*.

A boat captain that Hemingway befriended gave him a rare feline polydactyl—a cat with six and seven toes. Some sixty descendants of that gift now roam the grounds of his home and enjoy the celebrity benefits of being the only living vestige of Hemingway's presence in Key West. If I believed in reincarnation, I would like to come back as one of Hemingway's cats.

I could ramble into great detail about our snorkeling trip

to the coral reef where I became quite the mermaid, getting lost yet again on the way to the Miami airport, the delightfulness of the Drop Anchor Motel in Islamorada, which was exactly like the motels we stayed in when I was a vacationing child, and the flight from Memphis to Jackson on a stump-jumper when I was certain we would perish; but I won't bore you with the details. Four installments is more than enough for this journey.

When we arrived home exhausted on that late Thursday night, my husband finally admitted that he was glad we took our southernmost trip. Before sleep overcame me, I couldn't resist mumbling, "I told you so."

Phil and me at the southernmost point in the U.S.A. (2009)

a southernmost journey

OUR GRISWALD CHRISTMAS VACATION

The Clark Griswald family has nothing on the Rasberry-Napier clan when it comes to foiled vacation plans. Our trip to the Great Smoky Mountains had been in the works for weeks. We had planned everything down to the most intricate detail and had visions of ourselves relaxing in a hot tub after a day of taking in the sights, hiking and exploring. My beloved mountains, the place I journey to when I need to think happy thoughts, such as when I'm in a dentist's chair having a tooth drilled, would provide the breathtaking backdrop to a memorable holiday getaway. It's funny how we humans seem to forget that vacations hardly ever live up to the exaggerated expectations we have in our minds. As in this case, we forgot to factor in the Rasberry Rule—our adaptation of Murphy's Law—that always rears its ugly head when life threatens to flow smoothly.

Karen Clark Rasberry

Things did go smoothly for the first three hours, and I even let myself think that on this rare trip we might be able to somehow defy the Rasberry Rule. It was at a fork in the road in Birmingham where we made the fateful decision to take the bypass around downtown. It was the last day of November, and apparently that highway patrolman was dead set on meeting his monthly quota of speeding tickets. Since when do highway patrolmen drive unmarked, luxury SUVs with no bubble gum machines on top? In my opinion, that's a form of entrapment. He stealthily pulled up beside us, rolled down his window and zapped my son-in-law with his portable radar gun and then proceeded to zap every other motorist going one M.P.H. over the speed limit. About a mile down the road, there he was, outside his cruiser, waving all the once-happy travelers over to the side of the road for a special after-Thanksgiving surprise. A whole convoy of us pulled over as eagerly as if he were giving away free hams with every ticket. Like a leech with a zapper and a pistol, the officer sucked every bit of the holiday spirit right out of the car. For the next 200 miles, the lack of holiday cheer amongst us was in bleak contrast to the great expectations we departed Laurel with at 4:30 A.M. With the Christmas carols now mournfully absent from the radio, the only sounds were those of persons in obvious, worsening-by-the-mile respiratory distress. At the rate their health was declining, the Napiers would be in complete respiratory failure by the time we reached Gatlinburg. We were having so much fun that I wanted to cry.

  I would like to report that the ticket and the dastardly cold virus were the worst of it, but no, the Rasberry Rule had more surprises in store.

On the first full day, while sloshing around in the rain desperately seeking the Christmas spirit, we were heartened because the next day was predicted to be cold and sunny—perfect hiking weather for people with a temperature of 101 degrees. Even the news that Dollywood was closed for the rest of the week and that we wouldn't be able to see the amazing Dolly Parton Christmas show, was tempered with the knowledge that the next day, after a spell of years, I would return to one of my heart's homes.

With the other being the beach, Cades Cove is one of my top two favorite places on Earth. Being there, surrounded by the majesty of God's greatest creation, the tranquil cove soothes my soul on a very primal level. To understand the level of desperation that besot me when we saw the CLOSED sign just a few miles from the entrance, you need to know that I was just as determined to get inside Cades Cove as Clark Griswald was to get his family into Wally World. My subsequent tirade would have made him proud.

"No, we aren't turning around. No, no. We are going in if we have to bust through the gates and take the park ranger hostage. Do they not understand that this has been my reason for living for the past month? This is a full-blown, four-alarm holiday emergency here. We're gonna press on, and we're gonna have the hap, hap, happiest Christmas vacation since Bing Crosby tap-danced with Danny flippin' Kaye! I want whoever closed this park brought right here with a big ribbon on his head, and I want to look him straight in the eye and I want to tell him what a lying, no-good, rotten, low-life, snake-licking, dirt-eating, overstuffed, ignorant, blood-sucking, pig-kissing, brainless, hopeless, heartless, jug-butted, bug-eyed, stiff-legged, spotty-lipped, worm-headed sack of bear poop he is! Hallelujah! Holy hemlocks! Where's the Tylenol and cough syrup?"

There's not enough room here to tell you the rest of the story, but it involves a three-hour hike up a very treacherous mountain with no food, one bottle of water and a hip joint that locked up on one of us about half-way down the mountain.

I truly love the mountains with all of my heart, but there is no place like home for the holidays.

Phil and me on a hiking trail in the Smokey Mountains (2009)

Ben and Erin waiting at a Christmas shop (2009)

a southernmost journey

THE OLD CITY KEPT CALLING

When I first visited there in 1967 the city of St. Augustine, Florida was already four centuries old. It was in the summer of my twelfth year, and America had just recently celebrated its 191st Independence Day. Compared to the longevity of St. Augustine, our country was in its infancy, and I hardly existed.

When I think back to that adventurous summer when my father decided to systematically navigate the greater part of Florida in his new Chevy Impala, the Fifth Dimension song *Up, Up and Away*, is the soundtrack that fills my head. Even today when I hear that song it gives me a sensation of buoyancy and perpetual youth along with pangs of sadness. The melancholy comes from the realization that my parents were only 49 and 44 years old at the time—younger than I am now. I would pay good money to see them again in that relaxed, more-time-than money, vacation mode. I imagine my mother would be wearing colorful flip-flops, a crisp, belted sundress and Audrey Hepburn shades. I can envision the spry sailor with his cap cocked carelessly at an angle, perpetually tanned skin, dressed in typical tourist attire, passing out hard-earned dollar bills for us to blow on useless souvenir ashtrays and key chains.

It was the first and last vacation my parents ever took to St. Augustine and to that exotic, Spanish-flavored part of Florida. Although the span between my first and second visits was vast, the oldest city in America became a repository for my family's life story.

The ages have claimed many of the details of that first journey while some of them are as clear as the mythical waters of Ponce de Leon's Fountain of Youth. For years my sister and I would remember that trip with laughter and often returned to St. Augustine through the blotchy black and white Polaroid photos we took. Since Polaroid film was expensive and not as convenient as my daddy was led to believe when he purchased the camera, the pictures are sparse and deliberate. We are standing atop the centuries-old fort, Castillo De San Marcos, our unruly hair blown asunder in the Atlantic breeze. We are drinking from the Fountain of Youth, unsuspecting that Ponce de Leon had laid claim to an elaborate hoax in 1513. We are outside of Ripley's Believe It or Not Museum, a forbidding, Moorish mansion that contains a sideshow of afflictions, fat ladies, giants, shrunken heads and numerous open fireplaces. Daddy has a vacation-sized chew of Red Man tobacco in his cheek with nowhere to deposit his spittle. He assumes, believe it or not, that the fireplaces are spittoons for the patrons. We are as mortified by his actions as

a southernmost journey

the four-eyed Chinese man on display in the corner. In one picture my sister, mother, and I are aboard the red sightseeing train ready to chug through the semi-tropical, ancient city that had been omitted from the history books at Sandersville Elementary School.

Around 1996, when my husband had the opportunity to attend a continuing education course in St. Augustine, I was thrilled to tag along. The fort was just as I had remembered it and the sightseeing trains were still chugging along. The Fountain of Youth was still flowing and pushing bottles of its magical water. We found the same four-eyed Chinese man at Ripley's, and I noticed that the fireplaces had been boarded up—probably in 1967 after they found tobacco juice in every last one of them. Phil had also been there as a child and we agreed that it is a city that everyone should experience more than once. It possesses the perfect balance of history, natural beauty and quaintness—seasoned to perfection with a dash of exoticism and tackiness. Imagine a cleaner, older, more intimate New Orleans with Spanish flavor rather than French. We vowed to return and bring our children with us.

If I had known that thirty-five years after those Polaroid pictures were snapped that my unborn son and his wife would move there to fulfill their educational dreams, I would have been perplexed and amazed. If you had also told me that over the years the old city would call me dozens of times and that it would become my heart's home, I would have been filled with youthful skepticism.

After my daddy passed away in 2002, I found in his keepsakes a $1.50 ticket stub for the St. Augustine sightseeing train dated August 1967. Sadly, he didn't live to see his grandson earn his doctorate in physical therapy from the University of St. Augustine on August 13, 2004. Why in the world would he have kept that insignificant orange stub for all those years? He must have had a premonition as he was spitting in all those fireplaces.

The trolley ticket from my first trip to St. Augustine. It would cost $18.99 today.

Clark, my daughter-in-law Amanda (Sartin) Rasberry and Phil in downtown St. Augustine (2004)

REDNECKS IN PARADISE

The Alabama coast has become the destination of choice for thousands of southerners looking for rejuvenation from the salty air and to get a little sand between their toes. Because of its astonishing popularity with us average folks, it has been nicknamed the "Redneck Riviera." The first time I visited there was with a couple of girlfriends in 1979 right before Hurricane Frederic came through and devastated the area. Nature has a way of reclaiming what we think is ours. It was quaint, quiet, unspoiled, and the nearest grocery store was back up the road toward Foley. Little souvenir shops sold shovels, pails, Coppertone, and hermit crabs were my children's souvenir of choice. We bought at least a dozen and christened them all Kermit. It is where my children first got salt in their blood and started to wonder what was on the other side of that great big sea. In the beginning, there were still mom and pop motels hanging on to their piece of paradise, and modest, storm weathered beach houses where generations of families gathered to spend weekends in the sun and surf. Each time we went, familiar landmarks were either disappearing or modernizing. By the time my daughter was toddling around building sandcastles, condos were rising up from the white, sandy beaches.

If you have been there lately, you know that there is not much quaintness to be found unless you really look for it. For the most part, the owners of the weathered beach houses that happened to survive Hurricanes Frederic, Georges, and Ivan have sold their piece of paradise to developers. Twelve years ago, after twenty years of dreaming about a piece of paradise to call our own, we and two other likeminded couples took the plunge and purchased a condo. It was in the down market right after Hurricane Georges and we knew the risks, but we rolled the dice anyway. Hurricane Ivan almost destroyed our dream in 2004. After almost two years of hard work, sweat, and tears, we have bounced back better than ever. It isn't highrise or fancy, and we have to lug all of our gear across the street to get to the beach, but it fits us as loose and easy as a pair of old, rubber flip-flops. In the mornings, we can walk out to the docks on Ole River with a cup of coffee and wave good luck to the boats going out for the day's catch. When the setting sun casts its crimson net across the river, I take in a deep breath and smell the salty air. You never know what wildlife you might see in the river—herons wading gracefully, acrobatic dolphins, or pelicans diving in search of breakfast.

On occasion, the Blue Angels give us a surprise thrill when they fly over in formation on their way home to Pensacola.

All the other owners have become our friends, and in a sense, we are a small neighborhood doing exactly what people did 100 years ago on those waters. There is a surprisingly large contingent of Laurel owners in our twenty-seven unit complex, so we try to be on our best behavior. Some basically harmless indiscretions have prompted us to make a pact—"What happens in Orange Beach stays in Orange Beach."

Life remains dictated by the tides, the wind, and the waves. Fishing, boating, beach walks and swimming are the only things on our daily to-do list. In the early afternoon, children hear the magical calliope of the ice cream boat and scramble for coins to buy a cool treat. Later on, when the salty dogs return from the gulf with their catch, the neighborhood rushes to the dock to see what's for supper. The fish tales and scales fly as seagulls flock and squawk begging for some supper too. As the sun sets in the west and another day in paradise is winding down, somebody is always cooking under the gazebo by the river. A whiff of fish frying or burgers grilling is always an open invitation to come on down from the balcony and fix yourself a plate.

Most beachgoers don't realize it, but there is a whole other world to be explored in the bays and coves of the coastline between Mobile and Perdido Bay. If you head east by boat on Ole River past Ono Island, there are tiny islands where people camp, barbecue, and sun in chairs in the shallow brackish water. This is where you can catch a glimpse of one the legendary characters in the area. We call him the polka-dot man because he rows his red and white dotted skiff back and forth all day long in the summer wearing nothing but a loincloth. Everybody thinks his compass is a little off, but I think he's right on course. From there, we turn west toward Pirate's Cove where we can throw our anchor onto the sand for some live music and a cheeseburger in Paradise. It is legend that Jimmy Buffett penned his signature song there, but every burger joint in the south with a view of the water makes the same claim. I hope the easy unaffected beauty of the cove never changes.

On Ole River, markers warn "Idle Speed. No Wake." That rule applies to more than just boating. When we are at home on the Redneck Riviera, we slow down and don't make waves. There's no need to.

Phil, Clark and Amanda in the waters of the Redneck Riviera

a southernmost journey

SWEET ON ALABAMA

My daddy first took me to the Alabama beaches when I was too young to remember. The waves, sand and salty air must have gotten into my blood all those years ago. Following in that tradition, my little family has been vacationing in Alabama since way back when I could still wear a bikini and not embarrass the kids and other sunbathers. We even loved the beaches so much that we jumped in headfirst and invested in a condominium back in 1998 when prices were low. A couple of hurricanes, countless days of fun in the sun, and thousands of dollars in assessments later, I still argue with my husband that it's the best investment we have ever made. The amount we pour into it each year would definitely purchase us a vacation to any exotic locale we choose, but owning a little piece of Alabama is priceless. That's because I'm sweet on Alabama.

It first occurred to me when I noticed they have the coolest car tags in America. Though other Southern states lay claim to the title, no other is brazen enough to claim that it is the genuine "Heart of Dixie." And, isn't *Sweet Home Alabama* by Lynyrd Skynyrd just about the most inspiring anthem ever recorded? Even if you've never set foot in the state, grooving with that funky back beat makes you feel the need to get there as quick as you can.

Don't get me wrong, because there aren't any flies on Mississippi. We've got our own special attributes—magnolias, sweet tea and some very distinguished people who sprang up out of the Mississippi mud. We still say please and thank you. People still pull over in respect for funeral processions. There's not a heartache we can't fix with some good home cooking. We love momma, Jesus and America, and will fight you if you say anything untoward about any one of them. Mississippi is the birthplace of Elvis, for crying out loud. So why am I so sweet on Alabama?

To begin with, it's the only place I've ever visited that I wasn't in a hurry to get back home. Maybe that's because Mississippi and Alabama are like long-lost relatives who don't get to visit with each other that often. You get there and start to visiting, having a big time frying the catch of the day and boiling shrimp, and it's just one big, happy family reunion.

Both states are as Southern as it gets, but Alabama peppers the gumbo a little differently, and puts its own twist on being Southern. Mississippi has The Coast with casinos and world-class entertainment, but Alabama has the Redneck Riviera. We've got Brett, Archie, Eli, the Rebels, the Bulldogs and the Golden Eagles;

but they've got Bart Starr, Joe Namath, Bear Bryant, the Crimson Tide and the Tigers. We yodel with Jimmie Rodgers, but they croon along with Hank Williams. Mississippi gets down and blue with B.B. King, but Alabama jazzes it up with Nat King Cole. Alabama likes to claim Jimmy Buffett, but he was born in Pascagoula—so I say Alabama should back off. They've got Bob Riley. We've got Haley Barbour. In many respects the two states are about even, but it doesn't matter. I love Mississippi, but I've still got a thing for Alabama.

Perhaps my infatuation is simply green-eyed jealousy of our good neighbor to the east. It's sort of like when we were back in school and there was always this one girl that you really liked a whole lot, but you couldn't get a leg up on her no matter how hard you tried. She was just as nice as pecan pie, but you still hated her just a little bit. If you made an A on a test, she would score an A+. If you liked a boy, he would always end up asking her to the dance. If you were named to the top 10 in the beauty pageant, she would walk away with the crown. Her hair was always naturally blonder and straighter and her legs were a little bit longer than yours. You remember the kind.

Even with all of our great attractions and natural beauty, famous entertainers, legendary athletes and historical figures, Mississippi often finds itself following on the coattails of Alabama. I'm sure they thank God everyday for Mississippi, because without us, they would find themselves at the bottom of the list in a couple of undesirable categories. They aren't the fattest people in America, because we love our all-you-can-eat buffets more. Neither are they the poorest, because we hold that unwelcome distinction. All is not lost because I did find at least one category where Mississippi comes out on top. We've had four Miss Americas and they've only had three.

So what do I plan to do about this huge infatuation with Alabama? For as long as we can keep forking over assessments, for a few weeks out of each year, I can know what it feels like to be that long-legged beauty queen with straight blonde hair.

My first trip to the beach with my sisters: Phyllis Holder and Marilyn Maddox.

a southernmost journey

A VERY CRUDE AWAKENING

With the humidity hanging as thick in the air as the Spanish moss that hangs from live oaks down in the Louisiana bayous, along with the threat of yet another round of tornadoes in Mississippi, this past weekend gave me that all too familiar helpless feeling that we all get when a hurricane is looming in the gulf. This time it's not the threat of wind and rising water. From Grand Isle to Pensacola and other locations where the Gulf Stream flows, a sense of doom has settled over the coastline. Like the wrath Mother Nature inflicted upon us during Hurricane Katrina, this man-made river of oil bleeding from the bottom of the ocean is no less terrifying or destructive.

  This impending disaster may even be more so because we know what happened in 1989 after the Exxon Valdez spilled 11 million gallons of oil onto the pristine coastline of Prince William Sound. At least 1,300 miles of shoreline were affected. Environmentalists can only guess at what effect the spill had on wildlife, but some estimates are staggering—250,000 seabirds, 28,000 sea otters, 22 killer whales and billions of fish that are so vital to the fishing industry. Twenty years later, oil can still be found on the coastline and many of the species of wildlife are still in the recovery phase. Several species disappeared altogether. At least the Exxon Valdez spilled a measurable amount of the thick, black crude oil into the water. As of this writing, the Coast Guard claims that the ruptured well is still spewing 220,000 gallons daily into the Gulf of Mexico. While we wait for another form of Black Death to arrive on our coastline, they are still trying to figure out how to stop the flow.

    As I watch the news coverage of this slow-motion disaster, the optimistic side of me hopes that the economic and environmental impact will be minimal and even that the oil slick will disappear altogether. The pragmatic side of me knows it's next to impossible to even clean oil off of a carport much less mop up millions of gallons from hundreds of miles of sand. Just pour a quart of motor oil onto your kitchen floor and see how long it takes to clean it up. The selfish, fatalistic side of me is worried sick that my personal piece of coastal paradise will never be the same. If this spill is as bad as predicted, all I will have left are decades of memories to remind me of the way things were.

    The first time I visited Orange Beach and Perdido Key was with some co-worker girlfriends back in the mid-seventies. Highway 59 to Gulf Shores was just a two-lane road that interrupted the

a southernmost journey

sleepy towns of Loxley, Robertsdale, and Foley. Back in those days, there were no expressways, outlet malls, super service stations, highrise condos, or traffic. There was no such notion as "The Redneck Riviera" as travelers often overlooked Gulf Shores for the more popular beaches in Pensacola. A few mom and pop motels with VACANCY signs begging for travelers to stop, and a couple of souvenir shops peddling seashells, Coppertone, and cheap sunglasses were the only indication that the beach was a few miles due south. The beach houses were mostly weathered clapboard cottages safely perched atop stilts, built by families as fish camps and weekend getaways.

Today, Orange Beach is a world-class destination with glitzy resorts, island mansions, and endless family entertainment. There is very little evidence of the laid back fishing village that I fell in love with all those years ago. The vacationers and developers eventually descended onto paradise because a place that beautiful and pristine can't be kept a secret for long. Even so, sanctuaries for the mind and soul still exist, especially if you love boating and know where to go. The National Seashore east of Gulf Shores has sand so white and water so turquoise blue that it can blind you if you aren't wearing sunglasses. Some of the best days of my life have been spent on and in those waters with my family and friends, barefoot and blistered one and all. For many of us, the Gulf Coast, with its beaches, briny rivers, back bays and bayous are a church with no building—only the water, salty air, wildlife, sand and sky.

To envision our summertime playgrounds awash in sticky black oil, the waves breaking like thick molasses onto the shore, the sugar-white sands saturated with crude oil instead of suntan oil, and littered with dead sea life rather than bathing beauties, tomorrow and for years to come, makes us sick to our stomachs. To imagine that I could be an octogenarian before my personal paradise is pristine again is a very crude awakening. I think I want to cry.

P.S.
On July 15, 2010, BP stopped the oil flow after 87 days. The long-term effects are yet to be seen.

all part of the journey

Karen Clark Rasberry

A THREE-DOG WINTER

According to lore from down under, a three-dog night is one so cold it requires three dogs to keep you warm. Folks, it looks like we are in for a three-dog winter. My 87-year-old mother-in-law says she can't remember a winter so cold. She has been my personal weather girl for the past couple of weeks and has taken great pride in announcing the glacial nightly lows and Minnesota-like daily highs on each subsequent day.

After doing some research on the signs of a cold winter in nature, I know now that the indications of an impending three-dog winter were everywhere. One of those signs is actually across the road in my neighbor's yard. A hickory tree, thick with rust-colored leaves that should have floated away months ago, perplexed me every morning while I was having my coffee. The Farmer's Almanac says if leaves wither and hang on, it signifies a frosty winter and much snow;

if leaves are slow to fall, expect a cold winter.

The almanac states that animals will grow a thicker outer coat before an abnormally cold winter. A few weeks ago, before this artic blast moved in, I was driving down the road and almost lost control when I saw what looked like a prehistoric wooly mammoth grazing in a pasture. It turned out to be a bull with a thick coat of shaggy hair and large horns. At the time I thought it was odd, but now it all makes perfect sense. The bull sensed it was going to be forced to stand in a pasture all winter in sub-freezing temps, so it grew its own fur coat.

The almanac says that spiders will weave larger, thicker webs higher above the ground. I hesitate to re-live this nightmare from last summer, but it is so relevant to our current frozen state of affairs, it must be told. One happy day, during the blessed heat of summer, I was walking across my breezeway and noticed what appeared to be a nylon rope leading from a chaise lounge chair to a very tall arbor vitae plant at the end of my deck. Upon closer inspection, I realized it was a tightrope spun by a monstrous spider that even the makers of the movie *Arachnophobia* could not have brought to the silver screen without special effects. All joking aside, it was deadly looking with red markings and was as big as my outspread hand sitting there in a web the size of a trampoline. After the initial horror, and suffering full-body convulsions for at least thirty seconds, I determined that one of us had to die. With a can of Raid for exterminating wasps and hornets in hand, I bravely swore that it wasn't going to be me. It took the whole can and much twitching on the spider's part, not to mention loud yipping and more convulsing on my part, but it finally relinquished its hold on the web and fell with a haunting thud onto the deck. As a result of that one encounter with a mutant jungle spider simply preparing for a cold winter, I am scarred for life. Really. Seriously. Forever.

According to the almanac, squirrels will begin storing nuts early and busily before a hard winter. That's a reliable fact. It started back in the late summer when the squirrels were practically giving each other concussions while scampering in and out of the pecan trees in our yard. My husband and my mother-in-law, who both had visions of me using the sweet meaty nuts for Christmas pies and cookies, became obsessed with stopping them. A lone gunman and an octogenarian with a cane were no match for the swarm of rodents that descended upon our land. Don't get all offended because we were murdering innocent squirrels over here on the east side of the county. Remember, they are rodents in the same family as plague-carrying RATS.

In preparation for a brisk winter, humans tend to store an extra ten pounds of subcutaneous fat to insulate them from the cold. Starting around Thanksgiving and not subsiding until after the New Year, we instinctively pack in extra calories in the form of holiday candy, cakes, cookies and pies. So, if you are among the ones who can't button your pants, it's simply nature's way of preparing you for the long, harsh winter ahead. There's no need to go to the gym just yet because all of the shivering you are going to do over the next three months will burn off the extra lard by Spring.

So, there you have it—some of nature's signs that we are in for a three-dog winter. Knowing them now, after the fact, is really of no value and similar to wrapping the pipes after they are frozen solid. In the future, at least we will know when to have some extra dogs on hand.

Me, my sister Marilyn and Erin in the front yard of my childhood home — The three dog winter of 2008

Karen Clark Rasberry

A TOY STORY

During the yuletide monsoon last Monday, I was browsing around in the new Tuesday Morning store—the best thing to come into my life since under-eye concealer—in search of a toy to donate to the Toys for Tots program. Sadly, it's been years since Santa left toys under our Christmas tree, so I didn't have a clue as to which are the "in" toys on every tiny tot's wish list. There was an array of Barbie dolls in a variety of scanty clothing ensembles and aliases. There was Princess Barbie, Butterfly Barbie and Ballerina Barbie. It was all so confusing that my head spun a little at the thought of choosing one. Then, it occurred to me that little girls might not play with dolls anymore. In fact, playing with dolls is probably as old-fashioned as playing jacks or tiddly winks. Little girls are much too busy and sophisticated to tend to a plastic brat. Plus, there is the issue with self-esteem, and owning a Barbie with such unrealistic proportions might cause a young girl to develop a poor body image when she gets older. In hopes of finding a more ego-friendly toy within my budget, I pressed on.

After deciding it might be simpler to buy a gift for a boy, I switched my focus to snips, snails and puppy dog tails. Dominos... perfect. Wait. Do little boys know how to add without a calculator, or for that matter, sit still long enough to play such a mundane game? I've read that there's a higher incidence of ADD in boys these days. It's strange to me that no child back in my elementary school days had an attention deficit that a paddle couldn't straighten right out. There was this one boy in my third-grade class named Ronnie Bob who never paid attention to his three R's because he was constantly impersonating a log truck in various speeds of locomotion. Jerry Clower used to tell a similar story about one of the Ledbetter boys, so I assume that back in the day every rural school in Mississippi had a Ronnie Bob. Everywhere Ronnie Bob traveled, he was content with making motor sounds with his throat and shifting imaginary gears as he went. He especially liked to put on the brakes; and all his theatrics and sounds of halting a loaded log truck were quite realistic. Anyway, he would put himself in high gear when running down the hall to recess and in idle when he was eating lunch. His motor was perpetually running until one day the teacher got tired of talking over the noise. She clapped her hands to get his attention and shouted, "Ronnie Bob! Please stop your engine right now or I'm going to bend you over that desk and paddle the stew out of you!" He further sealed his fate when he said, "I cain't, teacher, my carberater iz stuck!" She forthwith silenced his motor, but he dropped out of school way shy of elementary school graduation. I never knew what profession he entered after all that education he received, but I bet you all the pine trees in my front yard that it involved a log truck and a chainsaw.

Confused, and obviously ADD myself, I kept looking for the perfect boy's toy. Old Maids...no, don't won't to turn him into a sissy. Chinese Checkers...one of my favorites of all time, but he could ingest the marbles. A BB gun...heavens no. "You'll shoot your eye out!" A baseball and bat... a head injury waiting to happen. Monopoly...how I loved all those tiny game pieces, wheeling and dealing, money and getting out of jail free. Come to think of it, Monopoly reminds me too much of our government and might instill greediness in impressionable young minds. Candy Land. Perfect! There shouldn't be any liability issues with giving a delightful board game that teaches color recognition and reinforces good sportsmanship. If there is one thing we need in the world this Christmas, it's good sportsmanship.

Later that day, a group of my co-workers was reminiscing about Christmases past. We were products of a generation of children who got excited over a stocking filled with oranges and walnuts or a paddle ball or a yo-yo. BB guns, bicycles and Barbie dolls were the ultimate gifts—a symbol of dawning maturity and a right of passage for our generation. On Christmas morning 2009, children will find stockings filled with iPods and smart phones. For old time's sake, slip a yo-yo, marbles or some jacks in there with all that technology. It will give you something to do while the kids are texting their friends to tell them what they got from Santa.

BEAU – THE WONDER DOG

When our children were small we always had animals around our home. Just name a species, and it has probably been part of our family. Speagle was a mix between a wiener dog and a coon dog and was just about the homeliest creature you would ever want to meet. There was Kermit the hermit crab that lived quite a long life considering he was taken out of his natural habitat. It's really hard to tell if a hermit crab is alive or dead until you start smelling the stench of rotten sushi. And then there was Jaws the goldfish that happily swam in a bowl on the kitchen counter for at least a couple of years. His demise came the day after a birthday party where every child in attendance fed him—twice. After eating every last morsel that floated from the little hands above, he exploded. Not pretty.

Beloved dogs came and went—all victims of their own curiosity. They just had to see what was on the other side of the road at the precise moment large trucks sped by. There were cuddly cats that tried to find warmth in car engines and Michelangelo the turtle that became a Popsicle when his bowl was accidentally left out on the porch one freezing night. There was Ether the Easter bunny that we let roam freely about the house until he clawed every door facing in the house to splinters. As a side note, rabbit urine is so caustic it could be used to remove varnish from furniture. To keep Ether from further damaging the house, Phil converted Erin's outgrown playhouse into a bunny mansion that rivaled Hugh Hefner's out in L.A. He lived contentedly until he met a gruesome death that still gives Erin nightmares. And, there was sweet Lilly, the last in a long line of doomed pets.

Eventually, the pain of losing animals became too much to bear. We gave up on the idea that pets could live happily and safely in our care.

Along came Beau, the black lab that stole my heart and everything else he could get his chompers on. Clark and Amanda gave him to each other as a wedding present in 2002. He was only six weeks old when they married and struck out to St. Augustine, Florida, to begin their life together. He was a rambunctious pup who took to the Florida life like a duck to water. With each of our visits, he had grown by leaps and bounds until one day he was the size of a giant black walrus. Always in his heart, he was a lap dog and would charge at me like a rodeo bull let out a shoot. Then he would pounce onto my lap and proceed to try to love me to death with slobber.

His was often a lonely life with his parents away every day at school. To pass the time, he completely and utterly consumed two apartments and one house. He ate wood like it was Milk Bone...carpet like it was Gravy Train. Sheetrock, porch screen, rocking chairs, aluminum cans and even stucco went in one end and eventually came out the other. But, one look into those repentive black eyes melted their hearts and nullified any intentions of punishing him severely.

Labs love the water, but Beau took it to new heights. There was water, water everywhere in his first four years of life; and he enjoyed it to the fullest. Beach walks...marsh swimming...boat rides, pier jumping where he would fly through the air like Wonder Dog to catch a Frisbee repeatedly until he was exhausted and foaming at the mouth. I really believe he would have performed this feat to his own death.

Beau gnawed and waited for his parents to come home every day so he could embark on his next adventure. He sat loyally at their feet while they studied into the wee hours of the morning. I guess you could say Beau earned honorary doctorate degrees in pharmacy and physical therapy during his stay in St. Augustine. Four years ago they moved back to Laurel to live life inland with his four dog siblings.

If it's true that one year of human life is equal to seven for a dog, he and I are currently about the same age. For both of us, the years are taking their toll. His coat is not so glossy anymore, and he has lost a bit of his speed and agility. I guess that's the reason why he couldn't get out of the way of that delivery truck. His prognosis is guarded at this time. He might not overcome his injuries. If he does, he may even lose a hind leg. My heart is broken. I can scarcely think of anything else but those big, sad, begging eyes. So, if you believe in praying for all creatures, great and small, please say one for Beau—the Wonder Dog.

Clark, Beau and Amanda at Pirate's Cove, an awesome hangout for dogs and cheeseburgers in paradise.

a southernmost journey

MAKING PEACE WITH THE '80S

On January 20, 1981, while Ronald Reagan was delivering his inaugural address, 52 hostages held by Iran for 444 days were set free. As a dejected Jimmy Carter was on his way back to his peanut farm in Georgia, our new Republican president was being credited for the hostage release and proclaiming that "government is not the solution to our problems; government is the problem." Perhaps the current administration should study and learn from Reaganomics of the '80s. That aside, the dawning of the '80s was a time of great political and cultural change in America. That particular day is a blinding beacon in my memory because great change was being delivered (literally) into my own back yard as well. A large poultry corporation had just unloaded approximately 45,000 baby chicks into three broiler houses on our newly acquired poultry farm.

Karen Clark Rasberry

The '80s are remembered as the decade of acronyms for fashion and marketing to describe different demographics. Young urban professionals (Yuppies), double income no kids (Dinkies), well off older people (Woopies), Porsche owning urban professionals (Poupies) and single women earning lots of loot (Swells). However, none of those applied to my situation in a lost decade that always gives me a hollow, lonesome feeling when I allow myself to return there. Great resentment filled me because I was not a Yuppie, Dinkie, Woopie nor a Swell. As a poultry growing, one kid, rural, no Porsche, young woman, mine was a lonely demographic. I was a Pornie. If the '80s had a fragrance, it would be the nauseating aroma of 45,000 chickens on a sultry, August evening. After a few years of pretending it was the smell of money in the air, each subsequent batch began to smell more and more like what it really was. So, you can understand why it is a decade that I am absolutely unable to look back upon and get a warm, fuzzy feeling.

Inspiration for this column came about when I stumbled upon a group photo of the Northeast Jones class of 1973 ten-year reunion. It took me a few seconds to locate and recognize myself among the ambitious faces of my classmates from thirty-six years ago. No small wonder. The person I finally determined to be me had a much fuller face than mine today and was camouflaged with enough makeup to make Tammy Fay Bakker run and hide. As is the case when I'm trying to impress others in social situations such as a class reunion, I was wearing black. Not an Audrey Hepburn-inspired cocktail dress but a one-piece, wrap-around halter, polyester ensemble with parachute legs and elastic ankles. To top off my

a southernmost journey

I-was-never-chosen-most-beautiful but was a darn-good-cheerleader fashion statement, my over-processed hair stands out as my premier what- was-I-thinking moment. Farrah Fawcett, God rest your soul, please forgive me for trying to imitate the most revered head of hair of all time.

The decade was a hodgepodge of forgettable fashion trends, overdone country home décor, Glam Rock and Thrash Metal. That's the decade that I was forced to develop an appetite for country music—-Conway Twitty in particular. It was *Tight Fittin' Jeans, Love to Lay You Down,* and *Hello Darlin,'* around the clock on the chicken ranch. The twang and growl, lonesome steel guitars, and the don't-come-home-a-drinkin'-with-lovin'-on-your-mind lyrics fit my position in life to perfection. If I was going to be forced to wallow in chicken litter, then I might as well do it with the bravado of Loretta Lynn.

As a Pornie, most of my time in the '80s was spent trying to keep chickens from freezing, scorching, dehydrating and fatally overeating. The rest of the time was spent disposing of the ones that died of heart attacks brought on by gluttony and genocide administered by my own two dainty, calloused hands. My only life outside the farm was spent in carpool lines, in the bleachers of T-ball baseball fields with my son or burning calories in dance aerobics classes.

My fashion sense was ruled by the trends of the masses and was one of big hair, shoulder pads, glittery tights, leg warmers, Reebok, "mom" jeans and denim jumpers. At the ripe old age 29, the glam life I once envisioned had turned into chicken litter. One minute I was a carefree, college cheerleader living off daddy's money and the next I was a married woman with a son and 45,000 stinking, clucking chickens to tend.

Mercifully, smack dab in the middle of the decade, the tide began to turn a bit. My hair became smaller and my abdomen became much larger. Pregnancy was the only excuse I ever found that could parole me from the chicken houses. The one redeeming thing to come out of the '80s other than Reaganomics and a few good movies, was a daughter to go along with my son.

With the passage of time, I am beginning to make peace with that pungent decade of tackiness. All that remains of my poultry-farming nightmare is a third of one of the chicken houses where we store junk and other unredeemable items. Only when my husband tears down that last fowl remnant of horror will I finally make my peace with the '80s.

Mom jeans, big hair, one child... must be 1985! Clark and me at Disney World

TELL ME THIS WON'T HAPPEN TO US

A forwarded email from Mrs. J read like this: Two elderly ladies had been friends for many decades. Over the years, they had shared all kinds of activities and adventures. Lately, their activities had been limited to meeting a few times a week to play cards. One day, they were playing cards when one looked at the other and said, "Now don't get mad at me…I know we've been friends for a long time, but I just can't think of your name! I've thought and thought, but I can't think of it to save my life. Please tell me what your name is…." Her friend glared at her for what seemed like an eternity. Finally she said, "How soon do you need to know?"

I thought the email I received from my "wallpaper" friend was quite amusing and way out of the realm of possibility until my phone rang a couple of nights ago. Of course, it was she on the other end rambling on about her latest treasure find at Earth Chic, a.k.a. known as Dirt Cheap to the B.B.B.B (Blonde Bombshell Bargain Babes). I am in a backslidden condition as far as my bargain hunting and need to experience a bit of revival in that area of my life. After a couple of trips into Earth Chic that left me unfulfilled, I decided to give it a rest until one of the B.B.B.B. tell me they have found the mother lode of bargains.

Mrs. J just celebrated her 60th birthday and has now become much older than me. Earlier this year, she also became the only grandmother in the world, which makes me the only unrelated grandmother in the world to little Connor Seth. Being an unrelated grandmother has its benefits. In my role as an unrelated grandmother, I can enjoy the experience without all the muss and fuss, such as wearing spit-up as a daily part of my wardrobe. Since Connor was born prematurely and not much bigger than a biscuit, watching him grow into a full-sized toddler has been very exciting. As a make-believe grandmother, it is my duty to tell you he is a sport model baby boy who already flirts and bats his killer blue eyes at all the baby girls.

Although Mrs. J is quite sprightly for sixty and is holding up well considering we have had to cut back on our beauty regimens because of this horrid recession, the phone call the other night has made me concerned that the email joke could happen to us sooner than I thought.

In case some of you didn't read the previous column entitled, *Friends, Good Friends and Wallpaper Friends*, Mrs. J is one of those friends who has been with me through the good, the bad and three ugly wallpaper hangings. But, her phone call and subsequent request has me troubled. I gave her a little leeway since grandmothers often do quirky obsessive things for their grandchildren, but buying a miniature 3-legged chair for $20.00 because it was so cute and cheap is bordering on the edge of questionable.

Her alibi went something like this. "You know you told me to go up to the new car wash on 16th Avenue because they were giving away free $7.00 car washes. Well, I did, but all that water and brushes going round and round kind of got me disoriented. Then it squirted all that purple, pink and blue soap on the windows. It reminded me so much of the psychedelic '60s that I had a flashback and thought I was inside a giant lava lamp. Honestly, I don't even remember driving to Earth Chic. The next thing I know, I'm putting the 3-legged chair in the car. I'm afraid I've turned into my mother. She wouldn't buy a chair unless it was missing at least one leg."

Her pitiful plea for help in turning the tri-legged bargain into a four-footed heirloom was even more heart rendering than when she begged for help with her wallpaper "situation." Without my help, she implied that the purchase of a perfectly useless, three-legged chair for $20.00 in order to save $60.00, would be the equivalent of burning a rolled-up Alexander Hamilton to light a fire—an act that could cause Mr. J's eye to start twitching uncontrollably.

The covert transfer of the chair into my car was a bit complicated, but we succeeded without being busted. Thanks to my skill with a screwdriver and drill and a new set of precious bun feet, baby

Connor will now be able to sit in his new chair at Christmas without fear of toppling over and busting his cute little, tow-headed noggin.

The next time she calls wanting me to get her out of a pickle, I think I'm going to fake it and tell her I don't recall ever knowing a Mrs. J, and then hang up.

Cheryl Jordan (Mrs. J) and me after playing a round of golf with B.J. Thomas. Yes, the "Raindrops Keep Falling on My Head" B.J. Thomas. (early 1990s)

ONCE MORE TO THE LAKE

me and Aunt Becky Gooch at Lake Bounds (2010)

Yesterday was exactly the kind of blistering summer day that my Aunt Becky would have loaded us kids up and headed to Lake Bounds. There has been quite a bit of reminiscing lately about Lake Waukaway, which prompted me to take a sentimental journey to another haven of bliss from my early childhood. Only this time, I traded roles with my aunt and became the chauffeur instead of the passenger. Although we didn't pack a picnic or bring a watermelon to chill in the icy spring waters, or have any inner tubes stuffed in the trunk, we carried hearts overflowing with memories of our special summer place.

    My sister, Marilyn, Aunt Becky and I took our journey down the winding country roads that we have traversed so many times. I searched for landmarks along the way that meant we were getting nearer our destination. The rickety wooden bridge just outside of Eucutta is long gone. The store in Eucutta where would stop for Popsicles and Dr. Peppers is closed. Old home places that appeared grand and haunted when I was young have been raised—replaced with trailer homes. Nothing along the way looks the same as it did through eyes that were once only a decade old. But, we wind and twist and laugh our way into the past. All three of us are amazed at the brevity of minutes, hours, years, decades, half-centuries, and life.

With no signs or fanfare, we finally reach the road to the lake. The virgin pines have been scalped from the land. The pine saplings make the entrance look unwelcoming and stark. We fear that the road to the lake is no longer shaded by a canopy of trees that gave it an air of mystery and antiquity. We climb a small hill and on our descent find that the forest and the atmosphere surrounding the lake have been spared by loggers and time. It is just as it was the last time we left it. I was so overcome with joy that I stopped the car in the middle of the road. For a few seconds I was ten again...and about to go swimming.

It's strange how childhood memories always magnify places, people and things. The water by the spillway that flowed into the gristmill wheel was once waist deep and filled with danger, but now it seems so shallow and harmless. Adults always warned us not to swim too close to the concrete tunnel of the spillway because it might suck us into the abyss of the mill.

While my memories of swimming at Lake Bounds are more juvenile and are seasoned with candy bars and ice cream from the lake store, my sister's recollections are of forbidden love and sweet first kisses. Her first crush was a bit older and had a reputation for driving fast cars and breaking hearts. She never really did forget her summer romance with a boy our daddy forbade her to see. We stand together on the dam thinking separate thoughts...the what might-have-beens and the wish-we-could-do-it-all-agains.

I just had to know if the water was still cold enough to turn my lips purple, so I shed my sandals and waded in up to my knees. No...I don't think it's nearly as cold...but my lack of hormones makes everything feel much hotter these days. I thought about diving in, clothes and all, but that would have been a silly thing for a middle-aged woman to do.

We didn't want to leave...ever...but Aunt Beck was patiently sweltering in the car. It seems she was always waiting and warning us to get out of the water because we had to go home to the real world. This trip to the lake was no different, but I think she realized how important a role she has played in our lives. She also remembers what a magical time and place it was. We helped her out of the car and made a few more pictures for posterity. It was a fine day for all three of us.

Phyllis and my cousin Randy Gooch at Lake Bounds (1955)

Karen Clark Rasberry

THE HOUSEDRESS

May has arrived in all its glory. With it comes graduations, sweet dreams of summertime, and Mother's Day. As I've shared in this column before, Mother's Day is never quite the same after your own mother passes away. This past week marked the fourth year in a row that I momentarily wondered what I should get her. There is a void in my heart that I suspect will never be completely filled, but with each passing Mother's Day, precious memories have begun to fill the empty space and push the reality of her absence into a happier place.

Predominantly in my memories, my mother is outside in the sunshine—fulfilling her duties as the queen of her small domain. If she's not bent over with her derriere straight up in the air digging in the dirt, she has a water hose in her hand furiously watering the plants, grass, me, or even the dirt in the driveway—an act that she claimed kept the dust in the house down. Seeing as how we lived alongside a dirt road that passing cars kept in a perpetual fog of orange dust, her chore seemed to me as futile as bailing water out of a sinking ship with a thimble. Colorful blooms spill out of dozens of pots she has placed strategically around the yard. She never was picky about what type of pots she planted her flowers in. From old wash pots to antique teapots to chamber pots, no vessel with sides and half a bottom was safe from her green thumb. In my recollections she isn't wearing cocktail dresses, Jackie Kennedy knock-offs, pearls or high-heeled shoes—for that type of apparel had no business in the closet of her post-war, rural housewife world. When I conjure up childhood memories of my mother, she is almost always wearing a housedress.

If you are of a certain age, you remember the humble fashion statement I'm talking about. They were sewn from an array of simple fabrics, were loose fitting for ease in tackling inside and outside chores, cool and breezy for the hot summer months and characterized by their easy front closure. Housedresses were considered matronly until some of the sex symbols of my mother's generation were seen wearing them on the big screen. Sophia Loren in a modest housedress was far more fetching than one of today's emaciated starlets walking the red carpet half naked in a designer gown.

The housedress is closely associated with the concept of housework and domesticity. At the same time, it is distinguished as not being a uniform, thanks in particular to decorations such as rickrack and appliqués. Not surprisingly, there are a number of race, gender and class insinuations all wrapped up in this innocent garment. For example, to be a housekeeper in a hotel was on the low end of the status spectrum, while a housewife of the '50s enjoyed great status.

Housedresses evolved over the decades, but they always knew that their place—just like the women of the day— was in the home. Although she never wore this version, there was a floor length adaptation called a hostess gown. How glam! Some styles were even sold with a matching oven mitt that housewives could hang on their belts—the ultimate in style and convenience. They eventually morphed into a boxy silhouette that made it appear that the lucky lady of the house was wearing a tent with pockets rather than an actual dress.

Feminists consider the housedress a symbol of oppression straight out of an archaic era. Hogwash. Today's runway and Hollywood-inspired fashions are absolutely more oppressive than a comfy cotton dress ever was. If you want to offend me, just pour me into a pair of matchstick jeans and force my aching bunions into a pair of stilettos. If you want to oppress me, just stuff me into a spandex dress with a strapless bra and a thong. If you want to nauseate the world, dress me in a midriff-bearing t-shirt and brand me with a butterfly tattoo. Today's fashion trends fail to make me feel desirable, powerful or the least bit liberated. They make me feel imprisoned, utterly ridiculous and of a mindset to burn down the nearest Frederick's of Hollywood.

As a gift to my mother, I bought myself the boxiest, most unflattering housedress I could find. If you see me around town, you will recognize me by the smile on my face and the free and easy way

I sachet down the street. However, I won't be waving at you with an oven mitt on my hand.

You never know. An oppressive symbol of the '50s just might become the most liberating fashion statement of this century.

My mother, Helen Jacqueline Clark, watering the yard in her housedress. This is exactly the way I remember her.

Karen Clark Rasberry

MY LIFE IN HIGH FIDELITY

Christmas came early the day after Thanksgiving when my sister, Marilyn, came through the back door literally bearing pieces of the past in her hands. You might remember my column from a few weeks back titled "A House Painted White." All that now remains of our ancestral home is a chimney rising out the ruins like a monument to the past. For the first time in my life, the old house was not there to welcome me home on Thanksgiving. I immediately thought of the greatest movie of all time and how the prologue proclaims that the old ways of the South are *Gone With the Wind*. It had never occurred to me before the house was demolished, but over my entire life, the old white house has been my Tara. Just as Scarlett O'Hara longed to return to her beloved home and family when war was raging and Atlanta was burning all around her, it was the place I would have returned to if faced with a similar doomsday situation.

Saved from an obscure closet in our Tara, my sister presented me with a musty stack of vintage record albums with the covers still intact. Thankfully, she is a pack rat who files things away with a disorganized system only she understands. If she has something I need, she may find it next week or next year, but she always finds it. I didn't give the old high fidelity albums much thought until later that night, when I realized how intimately they had influenced my life and have even served as the wellspring of inspiration through the years. Although there were several, it's safe to say I was willfully indoctrinated at an early age with at least three of the albums that are now in my possession.

On the very top of the stack of musical propaganda, a Deluxe Souvenir Edition of the original score of *Gone With the Wind* takes me back to the first time I ever heard *Tara's Theme* on the silver screen of the Arabian Theatre. The worn album cover has been Scotch-taped at the seams, and even the tape is peeling away, but fiery Scarlett and the heroic scoundrel Rhett will remain ageless and timeless characters in a lifetime filled with mostly forgettable movies.

The next high fidelity reminiscence in the stack was Elvis staring directly at ME with his dreamy blue eyes and that ever so slightly curled-up lip. Immediately, I am transported to the floor of the living room of my childhood home where I am lying with the album cover pulled close to my heart. Elvis croons, "Wise men say, only fools rush in...and I can't help falling in love with you..." I removed the album from the cover and inspected the tiny grooves under the kitchen lights. Yep, it was still there—a deep needle scratch on side one that runs from song #2 to the smooth inner circle that surrounds the RCA Victor label. I spit-shined it and applied album oil with a tiny brush repeatedly, but it never stopped skipping. Despite that perpetual annoying skip in the lyrics, I listened to *Blue Hawaii* at least a thousand times. Time passed. Eight-track tape decks replaced phonographs and albums. I filed *Blue Hawaii* quietly away into the depths of my memory.

The last album took me back to a leaden November sky in 1963. Grief seems to hang in the air about Sandersville School where I am a third-grader. Teachers are weeping openly and we children are bewildered and frightened by the incredible, devastating news that engulfed the rest of America. The album cover was once stark white but is now yellowed with age, and bears a simple sketch of John Fitzgerald Kennedy and these words—*The Presidential Years—1960-1963*. On the back, my daddy has penned the date that he purchased it to remember the life of a man whose path, except for wealth, privilege and fame, paralleled his own so closely. Even now, so many decades later, the events of that weekend mesmerize me. Last weekend was the 46th anniversary of the assassination. As always, I was held captive by the new documentaries airing on cablevision, watching with as much shock and disbelief as if it had just happened and the year were still 1963.

Reading an excerpted memoriam from Robert Frost at the bottom of the album helped me to put life's changes and the rapidity of time in perspective. *"And time persists, time that is both dark and light and forever changing. And nothing cherished ever wholly perishes.*

Gray November is a passing thing, and year's end is no end at all, but another marker on the great rhythm...Man, with his capacity for shock and grief, but also with his inheritance of faith, of belief, is participation in the great truth of continuity."

Phyllis, mother, Marilyn and me at JFK's assassination site in Dallas, Texas (1965).

Karen Clark Rasberry

A CARD FOR MY MOTHER

As many of you know, Mother's Day is never quite the same after your mother passes away. Just as my own mother did, I do not make a big deal of or expect expensive gifts from my children. Whether by providence or as a result of something I did, my children have given me the greatest gift of all. They have achieved their goals, married wonderful mates and have become productive, God-fearing members of society. They have provided me more joy than sadness, more satisfaction than disappointment, more laughter than tears, more reassurance than doubt; and the ability to love unconditionally, uncontrollably, and more deeply than I ever imagined was possible. If necessary, I would not hesitate to exchange my life for theirs. It takes becoming a mother to fully appreciate the wisdom and selfless sacrifices of your own mother.

My mother was a gentle soul who gave freely, laughed often, cried infrequently, loved us deeply and expected nothing in return. She was a simple woman who had no use for expensive jewelry, fancy cars or fine clothes. Her china and silver was a mismatched menagerie bought at grocery stores with savings stamps or found as a bonus in boxes of clothes detergent. Although she took pride in her appearance and never went to town before applying her crimson lipstick and Maybelline eyes, she seldom treated herself. Her only credit account at Fine-Brothers Mattison was always revolving when one of us just had to have the latest trendy item of clothing. She had the greenest thumb for miles around and delighted in sharing cuttings with her friends.

My most frequent and vivid memory is a vision of her watering hydrangeas, petunias and coleus scattered throughout the yard. The summer sun is low in the west and casts long shadows across the green grass. I have a fruit jar ready to capture the glow of the fireflies that are twinkling in the edge of the woods. Mother's left hand is propped on her hip while she uses the entire right side of her body to oscillate the hose nozzle so fiercely that she grits her teeth. It seems as if she has found the plants are on fire and she must hurry to douse the flames.

When I think of my mother, I prefer to remember her in the late summer season of her life when she was still active and content with my daddy by her side, not the autumn that left her infirm and held prisoner inside a body that could no longer grow and tend her flowers.

If I could send her a card it would be covered in bright summer blooms and would include a customary Mother's Day wish. Inside I would write these words:

Dear Mother, You will be happy to hear that I finally repotted the cactus you gave me years ago. It is sitting in my kitchen window so I am reminded of you every day. The plant that you called the "Aunt Cootie" plant is surprisingly alive and well. I cut it back every winter like you told me to, and it always flourishes despite my brown thumb. It is the only plant that I cannot kill! I have beautiful red petunias hanging in baskets on my front porch that will wilt in no time. At least for now they are thriving. I have one hydrangea that puts on leaves but never blooms. You will be happy to know Erin married Ben last November. I am so glad that he was able to meet you before you went home. She carried a bouquet of antique white hydrangeas and a locket with your and daddy's picture from the day you got married. Clark is still so handsome and looks more like Daddy every day. He has an amazing imitation of Daddy that makes me think he is actually in the room with me when I hear it. It always makes me laugh to hear his booming voice again. You will also be relieved to know that I have cut back on my sunbathing. Yes, I'm still playing tennis, and no, I'm not getting too hot as you warned. I've also learned to make dressing but have given up on biscuits. We have a garden full of sprouting corn, peas, potatoes, tomatoes, okra, squash and figs galore. Lots of unlikely people are now planting gardens because of the bad economy. I wish we could sit on the porch and shell a bushel or two this summer, although I'm not looking forward to shucking all that corn. Your creamed corn was always the best. I've run out of space so I will close for now.

I miss you and think of you every day—not just on Mother's Day. Don't worry about us because we are not sad anymore. We only feel blessed because we had a wonderful mother like you.

Love you, Karen

My mother and my oldest sister, Charlotte Murray during World War Two.

THE SUMMER OF 1969

In the early morning hours of August 18, 1969, two of the most monumental events of the 20th Century were simultaneously coming to an end. One was the vision of four under-thirty entrepreneurs. The other came at the hands of Mother Nature. In upstate New York about 40 miles from the village of Woodstock, Jimi Hendrix was burning up his guitar while slurring the words to Purple Haze, his archetypical psychedelic drug song of the sixties. Several hundred miles south, the Mississippi Gulf Coast had been totally obliterated by the strongest hurricane recorded in the 20th Century. On that particular morning, I was thirteen going on twenty and quickly learning more about life than I cared to know.

Although, I was in tune with the convergence of 500,000 hippies to a music festival called Woodstock, my world was far-removed from those three days of peace and music. It was just as well since I know with certainty that my daddy would not have allowed me to attend even if Woodstock had taken place in my own granddaddy's pasture down the road. Disgusted comments from my daddy such as, "Those long-haired, dope heads are going to be the ruination of this country," and "that don't sound like music to me—sounds like a bunch of cats fighting in drum," was my cue to keep hiding the fact that I was smuggling 45 singles by Janis Joplin and The Band into my bedroom. On the other hand, when Hurricane Camille leveled the coast then blew through Jones County on that seemingly endless night, it was more than too close for comfort.

These two events actually came as no surprise when you consider all of the shocking events that had already taken place that summer and the fact that man had just walked on the moon. Certainly, no ordinary music festival or hurricane could follow on the heels of such an extraordinary achievement by mankind. Even so, some of the skeptics claimed that Neil Armstrong had taken his giant leap for mankind onto the surface of an Arizona desert. Doomsayers speculated that Camille was due to the fact that the Apollo 11 moon landing had somehow altered the Earth's atmosphere. God had never intended for modern technology to advance to such heights, so he taught us a lesson by sending a mighty hurricane that no man could control or predict.

In the summer of 1969, it appeared that the music and excesses of the counter culture on display at Woodstock was evidence of the massive decline in morality, along with the Manson murders, Teddy Kennedy's slip up at Chappaquiddick and the Stonewall riots in Greenwich Village when gay and lesbian rights came to the forefront of America's consciousness.

Also on the musical front, Elvis made his famous comeback and the Beatles exited stage left. Few years can claim three films in the top 100 of all time, but the summer of 1969 saw the release of

Easy Rider, Butch Cassidy and the Sundance Kid, and *Midnight Cowboy*, the first X-rated film to win the Best Picture award. Perhaps the events of that summer was simply the dawning of the Age of Aquarius when the moon was in the seventh house and Jupiter aligned with Mars, when peace guided the planets and love steered the stars. No. Scratch that theory. Peace wasn't guiding the planets forty years ago because American soldiers were dying everyday in Vietnam. Love was nowhere to be found in the race riots and anti-war protests that were taking place from coast to coast. In the summer of '69, my sister was a young bride who sent daily love letters to her husband in the jungles of Vietnam. He came back to the U.S. two tours later, but the summer of '69 set him on a wayward path where he never truly found his way home.

For me, the summer of 1969 was the beginning of the end of the age of innocence. Thirteen is a very impressionable age for every child of any generation. For the past forty years, I have ridden those images, sounds and emotions like a magic carpet. That one summer did more to mold me than the twelve years that preceded it or the forty that followed.

I never again looked at the moon without thinking that somewhere up there on its surface was an American flag placed by the hand of man. Since the summer of Camille, the prospect of a hurricane fills me with guilty excitement and an unhealthy fear at the same time. Much to the embarrassment of my children, the music of that summer lies sleeping in my soul, and when it is awakened, it never fails to bring me to my feet whether a dance floor is handy or not. Because of Vietnam, war became more than news reels to me as I witnessed up close and personal how it ravaged so many of the young men of my generation. *Butch Cassidy and the Sundance Kid* became the standard by which I measure great movies. As a result, my ability to be entertained cinematically was diminished.

The summer of 1969 has been called many things. It was a series of perfect storms and earthquakes in the music, entertainment, political, social, and civil rights atmosphere that shook us to our core and almost tilted the Earth on its axis in the process. Whatever it was, for better or worse, those few months changed our nation and at least one thirteen-year old girl forever.

Me and my mother on our front porch in the summer of 1969.

my civil war

Karen Clark Rasberry

ALL ROADS LEAD HOME

It is true that all roads lead home. Old U.S. Highway 11 is one road in particular that has not only led me home but taken me to places that still hold a treasured place in my childhood memories. Planned in the 1920's and built over a number of years, it runs 1645 miles south from New Orleans north to Rouse's Point, NY at the Canadian border. Way down in Mississippi, it rolls gently past Eucutta Road through the town of Sandersville.

It was back in 1966, that my daddy decided that he would turn right and head north on Highway 11 to Washington, D.C., for our annual vacation. For my sister and me, this was the second worst thing that could happen—right behind the end of the world. We had our hearts set on Rock City and Ruby Falls. When school started back in September, how would we ever explain that we vacationed in Washington? It took me years to understand and appreciate why he had to make the pilgrimage to our nation's Capitol. It was his duty to make us aware of the greatness of our nation and the sacrifices that his generation had made during World War II. That same feeling of trepidation came over me a couple of months ago when my husband decided that we were going to take a road trip through the Shenandoah Valley to Gettysburg, Pennsylvania. Similarly, my husband was on a mission to understand how five generations ago men were brave enough to march headlong into battle against their neighbors, brothers and friends. While my friends were cruising the Caribbean or lying under the Tuscan sun, I would be cooped up in an SUV with a man in search of Robert E. Lee. As it did in 1966, portions of Highway 11 would weave in and out of that road to understanding.

On our departure day, as I navigated north onto Highway 11, a heavy feeling of dread filled the car. "Don't be sad. It's only 970 more miles to Gettysburg," my husband chirped as he reclined in the passenger's seat with his Civil War book. With Mississippi in the rear view mirror, we pressed onward to Alabama. The next morning, when we rolled out of Sweetwater, Tennessee, we had Robert E. Lee in our sights and Johnny Cash on the iPod. "I've been everywhere man, I've been everywhere. I've been to Tuscaloosa, Chattanooga, Knoxville, Johnson City, Wytheville, Blacksburg, Roanoke, yeah I've been everywhere."

It was in Lexington, Virginia, that we exited the I-81 motor speedway onto the calmness of the old highway and caught our first glimpse of Robert E. Lee. As a bonus, we stumbled upon his brave counterpart, Stonewall Jackson. It was a Civil War historian's gold mine that made my husband teary-eyed as he gazed upon a life-sized statue of the beloved Confederate general lying in repose. Just when he thought it couldn't get any better, we found the burial site of General Lee's gallant horse, Traveler, and the jacket General Jackson was wearing the night he was felled by friendly fire at Chancellorsville. With the Blue Ridge parkway to the right and the Appalachians to our left, we cruised through the breathtaking Shenandoah Valley (the Bread Basket of the Confederacy) further and further north until we reached the Pennsylvania state line. At the welcome center, we set our Mississippi feet on Yankee soil for the first time. It was very fitting that my husband got behind the wheel and took us from Chambersburg following the same path that thousands of Southern boys marched on the way to their destiny at Gettysburg.

Oblivious to everything except what our battlefield guide was saying, I took several pictures of my husband as he studied the field where General Lee ordered Pickett to make his charge. It was a religious experience for him and the culmination of thousands of hours spent reading and studying the Civil War. Comprehending the bravery and sacrifice of the men, both Union and Confederate, still manages to elude us 150 years later.

Still in awe of what we had seen in Gettysburg, we meandered back to God's country down Highway 11 into Winchester, Virginia, where there was even more Civil War history than you could shoot a cannon at. When we finally saw the Mississippi welcome sign and the beautiful piney woods of Jones County, it was all I could do to keep from crying. With one week, several navigational errors, six hotels and 2,240 miles behind us, we exited at Sandersville back onto old 11 until it led us home.

The trip wasn't glamorous or trendy, and not many people care to see pictures of the Devil's Den or where Armistead fell. In the Gettysburg address, President Lincoln said that we would never forget what the soldiers did there in July of 1863. I must confess, there are at least two Mississippians who never will.

Phil and me standing at the Highwater Mark of the Confederacy in Gettysburg, Pennsylvania (2007). I insisted that he wear the Ole Miss shirt. Hotty toddy!

Karen Clark Rasberry

A SKIRMISH IN MY KITCHEN

You readers might recall a story from my earlier book entitled "My Civil War with Biscuits, Greens and Chitterlings." After a long spell without any skirmishes over those three throwbacks to the 19th Century, my most recent battles have been waged mainly over my husband's insistence that I cook all the vegetables that he himself personally planted, harvested, shucked, shelled and stored in the freezer. If all the time, hassle, and aggravation of seeing his garden grow from seed to freezer could be converted into dollars, I estimate he spent about $5,000.00 for $300.00 worth of food. That's really not a bad investment considering our past ventures in the stock market. His argument is that he gains self-satisfaction and a feeling of accomplishment from his gardening and compares it to how Leonardo da Vinci must have felt when he stood back and admired the *Mona*

Lisa. Since he enjoys playing in the dirt, hoeing, and hauling farm implements to the repair shop every few days; who am I to stand in the way of all that creative energy?

Last Saturday, I must have let my guard down, because I didn't see the attack in the works until it was almost too late. Ole Stonewall Rasberry and his brigade, which consists of our one and only son, were in full assault mode when I arrived home from showing a house. Nothing puts me on the defensive quicker than finding men messin' and gummin' (as my mother was fond of saying) in my kitchen. I believe I would rather have bats in my belfry or lice in my hair than two macho men meddling in my kitchen. It's strange to me how my husband, who doesn't even know how to put a dish in the sink or turn on the stove with the directions in his hands, can suddenly become an authority in the kitchen. Not to mention my son, who would have starved to death in his teens if not for my selfless sacrifices over an electric range, has suddenly re-invented the use of pots and pans. According to them, I have been doing things all wrong for the past thirty-five years. They just couldn't believe I had the audacity to rebel against their holding my kitchen hostage while using my pots, pans and utensils as their own personal weapons of torture. Their acts were no more honorable than when General Sherman stole all the Confederate livestock and then burned the barns.

If not for the presence of my son-in-law, the Methodist youth minister from whom I was still trying to conceal my Charles Manson side, the skirmish could have turned into a full-fledged massacre. All of a sudden, I heard the sound of cold meat hitting hot grease in an electric cooker. Within two seconds, the smell of pig excrement joined the aroma of collard greens boiling furiously on top of the stove.

"What is that smell? You can't really be cooking those in my kitchen!" I snapped. "Oh, come on mom, we'll miss the Rebels playing in the 3rd quarter if we have to cook them outside. They don't smell any worse than frying chicken would," fired the brigade of one. After a few rounds of rapidly firing adjectives that describe the smell of chittlins' frying, along with verbs to describe what I was about to do if my husband didn't step away from the cooker and drop the pig guts, the skirmish ended without any casualties. Ole Stonewall Rasberry waved a dishcloth in surrender then took his cooker of hot grease outside. Oh, there was one death. The angelic image that my son-in-law once held of me had been dealt a killing blow. He's been in the family almost a year, so it was bound to happen sooner or later. He now has a really good understanding of my stance on not cooking chittlins' in the house.

Since I always try to inject a little wisdom into each of my columns, there could be three possible morals to this story. To teach me tolerance and patience, it might be, "If you can't take the smell, get out of the kitchen." To teach my husband and son courtesy and give them a true understanding of the way things were meant to be, it should be— "If Mama ain't happy, nobody is happy." After the skirmish in my usually peaceful kitchen, the words of General Robert E. Lee ring the truest. "It is well that war is so terrible. We should grow too fond of it."

a southernmost journey

SPRINGTIME AT LITTLE MONTICELLO

It's been a long spell since you readers have had an update about the goings on at "Little Monticello." To refresh your memory, I nicknamed our home and spot of land this after Phil and I took a road trip through Virginia a couple of summers ago. My husband was so enamored with Thomas Jefferson's magnificent estate in Charlottesville and so inspired by the accomplishments of one of our founding fathers that he decided to live the remainder of his years emulating him. He has now entered his third summer in pursuit of this lofty goal. For the most part, I am a bystander in this 18th Century world he wishes to reincarnate, lending a hand only when my guilty conscience prods me into the dusty rows of his domain. Although his gardening skills have improved bountifully over the past couple of summers, my understanding of why he willfully breaks his back has progressed only minutely.

It is the terminology he uses when referring to the gardening process that confounds me the most. Listening to him speak this lost language in the 21st Century, with phrases that often sound violent, mildly obscene and contort the English language into an unrecognizable form, is mildly entertaining and a far cry from the familiar terminology of his profession. His diagnoses of my various and sundry pains, such as "Your sacroiliac is hyper-mobile from your two gestational experiences. The bursa in your greater trochanter is probably inflamed by the rubbing of the iliotibial band that runs down your femur. You need to maintain those strengthening exercises I showed you, " translates to "I'm too tired and give out to massage your back. Go do some leg lifts and it will feel better."

This bizarre language started again in the late winter when he longingly proclaimed that he would soon be able to "break up his garden." My first interpretation of this happy news was that he was going to "break up with his garden" and that his love affair with Thomas Jefferson was over at last. No such luck. It meant that his romance with dirt was about to be rekindled.

One evening he came putt putting through the back yard on his little red Farmall tractor and told me to hop up beside him because we were going to "stick" his beans. Why would he want to stick his butterbeans? I wondered. Have they threatened him with bodily harm, or are they sick and need some blood work? As it turns out, stick, when referring to beans, is a noun—not a painful verb. I caught on forthwith. Sticks are to butterbeans what trellises are to vines.

It was right after the arrest of Lawrence Taylor for his alleged dilly-dallying with a 16-year-old girl, when the most disturbing moment of the spring occurred. Phil came in the back door all sweaty and crimson-faced and confessed to his innocent daughter and me that he "needed to get some young whores" or he couldn't physically keep up with his garden anymore. With a look of utter shock on her face, Erin exclaimed, "Dadeee! That's disgusting!" She and I were relieved to remember that there is such a farm tool as a hoe and that a hoer is one who cuts down weeds so plants can grow unfettered. That's just one example of how ancient gardening terminology can skew our modern interpretation of the English language.

Just last week, he was in a huge hurry to get home from the beach so he could "dig his taters." At once, I had a hilarious vision of him grooving up and down the spud rows, playing imaginary bongos over his starchy tubers like a beatnik from the '60s. A vision of Dr. Phil diggin' them taters. Tell me that ain't funny.

Then one day he announced in a somber tone that he had just "laid his corn by." Confused, I inquired, "Did you lay amongst the corn rows to accomplish this or did you actually lay the corn by the side of the road or some other convenient place?" It seems that "by" used in this olden lingo is not a preposition but a noun—a spiritual place where corn goes to complete its purpose on Earth — analogous to when God-fearing souls go to the "sweet by and by."

A couple of weeks ago he had to go over to the garden to "cage his tomatoes." We all know how rambunctious those "Big Boys" and "Better Girls" can be. I suspect it's best to go ahead and lock them up while they are young so they don't get into too much trouble.

My husband says it won't be long before his luscious

"roastinears" are putting on silky, golden tassels. I'm not sure what to expect when that happens, but my imagination has gone wild over the terminology. It sounds more risqué than the can-can at the Moulin Rouge.

Phil at Thomas Jefferson's Monticello. The day my civil war began. (June 2007)

a southernmost journey

THE GARDEN STAGE OF LIFE

Last weekend, while up to my elbows in corn, butter beans, and tomatoes—all fresh-plucked from our very own garden, memories of my mother made the chores more bearable—maybe even enjoyable. A few weeks ago when Phil excitedly announced that his "roastin-ears" were tassling, I began steeling myself for battle with the husky enemy. Then I remembered how putting up corn was once a play where each member of our family had a very important role to play. During the summers of my childhood when the corn patch made its annual debut, life as we knew it came to a screeching halt. The cornfield show had to go on. When the corn was ready to be picked, there was no buying time or bargaining with it. There was no swimming, movies or diversions from the production at hand. Putting up corn was a monumental task that required many hands to process foot tubs full of the manna harvested from wretchedly hot and scratchy cornrows. My daddy starred in the opening scene as the cultivator. Everyone played supporting roles as corn huskers at one time or another. I was usually cast as the opening de-silker while my sisters, armed with Stanley brushes, filled the parts as encore de-silkers. My mother, who never failed to give Tony Award-winning performances, was the creamer, blancher and cooker of the corn. I can still see her forcing the golden ears up and down a concave wooden slat across its steel slicer. With corn splatters covering her face and glasses and everything within twenty yards of her, she battled the corn as if our very survival depended on her performance.

The process of turning seeds into steaming bowls of creamed corn for winter dinner tables, requires more sweat and toil than most people are willing to sacrifice. For years I argued with my husband, "Why go to all that worry and expense when the Jolly Green Giant can do it for us?" The sweet smell of the corn blanching, corn splatters and silks covering the countertops, and the stove stealing the coolness of my kitchen, all took me back to a kitchen where oscillating fans fought a losing battle against a gas stove and the June heat. For a time last Saturday, I slipped into the role I had seen my mother play so many times. It felt natural and instinctive there in the hot spotlight of my kitchen—the understudy mimicking the master.

Although my husband fears otherwise, we probably won't starve without all the vegetables we have stocked in the freezer. Fears aside, one bite of fresh creamed corn made me realize all the work has been worth the trouble. What you get from the Green Giant is edible and convenient, but you can't taste any love in what comes from those aluminum cans.

    I think what we are doing transcends our physical needs. It is out of the desire to do something that isn't common or expected anymore. Vegetable gardening really is a dying art form where you get to stand back and admire what you have created with your own hands. Unlike most other art, when you are done admiring it, you get to eat it. I believe it also fills our want for continuity and tradition. It fulfills a longing to commune with the spirits of our childhood and the ones who showed us how to perform on this stage of life.

KEEP ON KEEPING

My husband drives me crazy because he wants to keep EVERYTHING. I threw away a plastic gallon bucket that would have made a good colander. He dug it out of the garbage and scolded me for throwing away such a perfectly useful bucket. He found a ceramic flowerpot among the rubble around his daddy's authentic log cabin (on which he spent my Virgin Islands trip savings for a new roof). He was convinced that he had found a treasure that we could hand down through the ages. Although I'm certain the piece was mass-produced and sold at Kress decades ago, I told him to keep it somewhere out of my sight. Careless words flew out of my mouth and wounded his feelings when I snapped, "All that old what-not is good for is collecting dust. It's tacky and I don't want to keep it in my house."

Keeping is a way of life around here; and sometimes it does drive me crazy...all this fixing, renewing, reusing, saving...Sometimes I just don't feel like keeping things. I'm attracted to bright and shiny things that smell like new instead of like must and rust. I love the seductive cologne of new cars and the fresh paint and lumber incense of new houses. My husband declares that cars with less than 100,000 miles are barely broken in. I drive a new car off the lot with 26 miles on the odometer and immediately start coveting other sporty models that pass me on the road. Nothing makes me happier than buying a new outfit, while nothing pleases him more than wearing old jackets with outdated lapels and ties that went out of style with the Reagan administration. He didn't speak to me for a week when he discovered that I had sneaked his baby blue, Members Only jacket off to the Salvation Army. Another thing he insists on keeping are those high profile, mesh caps he gets free from local feed and seed stores and tire shops. In fact, it's the freebies, the orphaned objects and the white elephants that no one else wanted that he finds irresistible. I'm pretty certain he hoards and keeps and saves because he can't help himself, and because he has learned that it irritates me to no end.

A few days after the flowerpot incident, it occurred to me that I have been too quick to cast aside things that have lost their shine or don't fit in with my modern sensibilities. There is a feeling of continuity and connection to the past in driving an antique car or cooking in a half-rusted cast iron pot and sitting on the porch of a log cabin, hewn by hands that stopped toiling 150 years ago. It is the keeping of these needy objects that allows us to commune with souls who have passed before us. After my parents died and I walked into their house for the first time with nothing but silence to greet me, I realized that sometimes there just isn't any more...Sometimes what we care about the most gets all used up and goes away...never to return.

So, while we have it, it's best we love it and care for it, fix it when it's broken and try to heal it when it's sick. This is true for log cabins, Dutch ovens, old cars, holey buckets, outdated neckties and cheap flowerpots. Above all, it is true for marriages, old friendships, ageing parents and for children who may have veered off course.

This reality check bounced hard off my heart. I went out to my husband's workshop that also does duty as a chittlin' and fish cleaning area, to search for the dejected little flowerpot. Sure enough, there it was, perched high atop a cabinet, out of my sight. Even standing on a wobbly chair, I could barely reach it. It would have served me right if I had fallen and broken a bone or two. I blew off the dust, ran my fingers over the crackled glaze and began to see it in a whole new light. It could look terribly chic catching sunlight on my kitchen windowsill. So what if it is one of millions? Or, it could be one in a million. Regardless of its value, someone he once loved thought it was beautiful enough to buy. I vowed to keep it in full view as a reminder that some things, no matter how worn out, weathered or tacky, need to be held on to.

If there is a moral to this column, it is that we need to keep on keeping—no matter how irritating or inconvenient it is. We must fix broken relationships, renew old friendships, reclaim patience, and recycle love like it's going out of style. We should be cautious about what we cast aside. You never know when there won't be any more.

IN JEEP AND BUG LOVE

In 2004 when my ailing father laid eyes upon my daughter's first Beetle, his old WWII mentality wouldn't allow much of a compliment. "Well, I guess it's alright...for a Hitler car." By purchasing a Datsun pickup truck in 1969, he proved that he had made his peace with Japan for trying to kill him on numerous occasions. For reasons that had everything to do with the carnage he witnessed up close and personal on D-Day, he never got his wires uncrossed with the Germans. Daddy took Hitler's heinous deeds rather personally and refused to have any further dealings whatsoever with Germany. He even had to force himself to eat my mother's delicious German-chocolate cake. So, you can understand the disdain when his baby granddaughter drove up in Hitler's brainchild.

In 1937, Hitler met with Ferdinand Porsche to discuss his idea of a Volkswagen— or "people's car." He wanted it designed to carry 5 people, cruise up to 62 M.P.H., return 33 M.P.G. and cost only 1000 reichsmark. The car would be made available to members of the Third Reich through a scheme similar to a savings booklet. However, war started before large-scale production of the Volkswagen could get under way. The rest, as Beetle lovers know, is history. In 1972, due to its popularity around the world, the Bug shattered the world's single-car production record with 15,007,034, surpassing Ford's Model T.

In 1940, there was much concern about the victories the Axis powers were scoring in Europe and Northern Africa. Before we entered the fray, the U.S. Army put out a call to 135 automakers to develop a prototype of a four-wheel drive reconnaissance car and gave them only 49 days to do it. As a result, only two companies, American Bantam and Willys-Overland submitted a plan. After Bantam's design was chosen, the government enlisted Willys and Ford Motors to proceed with the mass production of the vehicle that helped win the war.

Although the origination of the Jeep name is ambiguous, it is synonymous with tough and dependable. It has been the transportation of choice for liberators and adventurers for seventy years. One high-ranking officer in WWII claimed it could do anything except swim or climb a greased pole. It's as faithful as a dog, as strong as a mule, and as agile as a goat. From the Battle of the Bulge to the dense jungles of Burma Road, the Jeep took American soldiers anywhere that freedom was threatened. The hoods doubled as chaplain's altars and card tables. The ¼ ton warhorses served as battle stations for generals and ambulances for the wounded. No other mechanical innovation was more instrumental in winning the war than the Jeep.

My daddy had already passed away by the time we were bitten by the Jeep love bug. I'm quite certain that he would have had a fine time reminiscing about his wartime Jeep experiences from the passenger's seat. He would have been pleased as punch over its fighting legacy from WWII. Since ours was built pre-Daimler, he possibly would have overlooked the fact that the Germans now own Jeep. I can just hear him now, "Aww sugar, this is a fine piece of machinery. We gave those Krauts HELL with this little buggy!"

When Erin and Ben drove up the other day in their new 1971 convertible, Super Beetle, it was impossible not to fall head-over-heels in bug love. Driving with the top down while listening to Janis Joplin is like riding in a tiny time machine. Behind the wheel, it is still the '70s, and I am a free spirit with flowers in my hair, headed to wherever the road might take me.

While riding with the top down in a Beetle is mostly about looking back, riding in a topless Jeep is primarily about looking forward. When shifting gears in my red CJ (civilian jeep), I'm a bona fide woman who has earned her stripes in the trenches of motherhood, wifedom and life. Driving with Buffett blaring on the radio and my hair whipping in the wind is like taking a drink from the Fountain of Youth.

While the stigma attached to the Volkswagen dissipated decades ago, it is difficult for me not to consider the paradox of the two automobile brands that we have grown to love. I would be remiss as the daughter of a WWII veteran not to appreciate the historical implications. During the most turbulent time in world history, the creator of one became the reason for the creation of the other.

If there had been no Bugs, there would be no Jeep love. If there had been only Bugs but no Jeeps, there would be no Bug love at all. Today, we would all be speaking German and eating sauerkraut; and everybody would hate driving their bug-like "people cars."

Our 1995 Jeep Wrangler and Erin and Ben's 1971 VW Beetle (lovingly named "Lucky").

a southernmost journey

WE'RE GONNA NEED A BIGGER BOAT

The ongoing news coverage of coastal mayors assuring tourists that the beaches are still open despite the oil that is lurking in the gulf reminds me of a distant 4th of July when Amity Island was being terrorized by a totally different menace. With a grafitti-enhanced billboard in the background depicting an enormous shark fin, the fraught mayor declares, "It's a beautiful day! The beaches are open." Of course, the oil threat is all too real while Amity was an imaginary island whose plight and iconic characters became so thoroughly engrained into our consciousness that it forever changed the way we look at the water... and movies.

Moviegoers didn't know what hit them...or bit them... thirty-five years ago when *Jaws* became the first ever summer blockbuster. Chances are the theme song is already building in your head. Duh-dum...duh-dum...You know it well. It's that tune you hear every time you go for a swim in the ocean—the one that sends the frontal part of your brain into primal fear overdrive. For a time, the notes were so haunting that I was even afraid to get in a bathtub full of water or sit on a toilet.

Up until the summer of '75, cinematic entertainment was very different than it is today. If nothing else, darkened theatres offered a cool spot where we could escape the vile heat of summer and gorge on buttery popcorn that couldn't be replicated at home. Summertime offerings were often so non-eventful that we never gave them a second thought once our eyes adjusted to the light of day outside the movie house. *Jaws* changed all that forever. Little did I know on that summer day when my sisters and I sped to a Hattiesburg theatre in an orange VW Rabbit, that it would spawn this column thirty-five years later.

Not many movies bite you in the opening scene and don't let go until the credits roll. We will never forget the tipsy girl who made the mistake of going skinny-dipping in the ocean in the dark—and the collective gasps that sucked the oxygen out of the theatre when the shark took his first bite from her dangling legs. It was jump-out-of-your seat shock. It was bloody and real. It was wonderful.

Steven Spielberg had the perfect seed for a growing a blockbuster in Peter Benchley's best-selling novel about a great white shark that was terrorizing a New England resort town. But, it was the seamless editing and a perfect cast of characters that grew it into a classic.

Robert Shaw, the tough-as-nails shark hunter, Captain Quint; Roy Scheider, the faint-of-heart Sheriff Brody, and Richard

Dreyfuss, the college-boy marine biologist named Hooper, were as an unlikely trio as you would ever see on the silver screen. Somehow their chemistry or the lack thereof worked like a charm. What they brought to the big screen was genius. It was comedy at its most sublime. It was drama and suspense at its best. We couldn't wait to see who the wily shark would eat next.

Nobody will ever forget the shock on Sheriff Brody's face or the words he blurted out when the less than realistic shark made his first appearance on screen. Subsequently, "We're gonna need a bigger boat" became the catchphrase we often use when we realize that the resources at hand are inadequate or when we find ourselves in situations we didn't quite bargain for.

The shark hunters' bonding moment aboard the Orca as they compared scars, and Quint's drunken monologue on the mission and the fate of the sailors aboard the U.S.S. Indianapolis were personally the defining moments of the movie. One of the greatest impromptu scenes in cinematic history became a catharsis of family history. I was just nineteen, and had never heard the tragic story of what happened to the Indianapolis after my daddy transferred off it. After keeping his war experiences bottled up for years, he finally confessed that divine intervention saved him from the fateful voyage that killed hundreds, left others to be eaten by sharks and put the flagship of the Navy at the bottom of the sea.

It would be embarrassing to say how many times our little family has re-watched *Jaws* over the last thirty-five years. As two men who share a love for the sea and fancy themselves as Hemingway types, my husband and son have formed a cult of two who have memorized every line and studied with enthusiasm the interaction between the villain shark, the protagonist and the two antagonists in the movie. They have even concocted a language consisting entirely of nuanced movie dialogue that they use exclusively in the realm of their father-son world.

To say that a movie that is now considered outdated by modern standards profoundly affected my family would be an understatement. To adequately explain this fixation, I would definitely need a bigger boat.

My daddy, QM 1st Class Ralph G. Clark, on the deck of the U.S.S. Indianapolis (1942).

to everything a season

Karen Clark Rasberry

THE DAY OUR INNOCENCE DIED

On September 11, 2001, New Yorker's woke up to a rare, unclouded day with a sky so blue and full of hope that it had to make them glad to be alive. Summer was in its waning days and even the leaves in Central Park must have been beginning to hint at the promise of fall. Looking back, there was an air of innocence in that day with the sky so perfectly brilliant and promising. It was the kind of day that you just don't expect your world to be turned upside down. Since that day has now become eternally etched into the American psyche, we all remember precisely where we were and what we were doing when we heard the news. It's actually quite amazing that on September 11, 2001, at 8:45 A.M., America still possessed some semblance of innocence and was secure in the notion that no foreign enemy would ever have the audacity or cunning to attack us where we live. As horrendous as it was, Pearl Harbor was different in the fact that Hawaii wasn't yet a part of the United States, and the attack by the Japanese was against our military installation and not civilians.

A mere sixty seconds later, when Flight 11 smashed into the North Tower of the World Trade Center, we desperately clung to that innocence and tried to block unthinkable thoughts of a terrorist attack from our minds. It had to have been a terrible accident. But the sky was so clear and the building so prominent in the skyline of the city, no competent pilot would fly a plane directly into it. As the sky began to fill with smoke and death, our hearts and minds began to cloud just a little with doubt and fear. If you watch the replays of the live footage from that fateful day, you can catch a glimpse of the murderers of our innocence flying toward us at lightning speed. There it is—a chilling, glint of another large plane taking aim at the South Tower, hell bent on killing as many Americans as possible. At 9:03, after seventeen minutes of desperately clinging to hope, we had no choice but to let it go. At 9:37, when Flight 77 flew into the Pentagon, our country went into a state of shock and disbelief. Many of us dropped to our knees in prayer. At 10:03, when Flight 93 was commandeered by a group of heroes and went down in a Pennsylvania field, we wondered if America could survive. We did, but life as we knew it was gone forever. That was the day that our innocence died.

As far as I know, I had never met a single person who died that day. The victims were like you and me—businessmen and women, firefighters, policemen, janitors, clerks, and cooks who woke up on a clear September day full of hopes and dreams. They simply went to work or boarded a plane then eternally became a part of history.

Cantor Fitzgerald was a brokerage firm located in the World Trade Center at the center of the world's money capital. They hired only the best of the best. That's why 658 employees were at their desks when Flight 11 smashed into the North Tower. For some of them death was instant. For others, death came by suffocation from smoke inhalation. The rest died when the building fell, like a stack of cards, until there was nothing but smoke, fiery ashes and melted steel. Out of the almost 3000 who were murdered at the hands of terrorists that day, 658 worked for Cantor Fitzgerald.

While the airplanes were hijacked by cowardly, worthless pieces of humanity, American heroes who value freedom and life were abundant on that day. When others were fleeing for their lives, firefighters, policemen, Port Authority workers and paramedics ran head-on and fearless into the burning and doomed buildings. Over 400 of New York's finest and bravest, many with Irish ancestors who came to America seeking freedom, died at the hands of a radical group that despises that same freedom. Since 9-11, the sound of bagpipes playing *Amazing Grace*, has become our national song of mourning. If there is any sound more haunting or heart wrenching, I'm not sure we Americans ever want to hear it.

It makes me enormously proud that the terrorists who hijacked Flight 93 underestimated America and the heroes on board. The passengers and crew, who were small in number but mighty in bravery, have been forever immortalized in books and movies. Todd Beamer's last words, "Let's roll," became the catch phrase and rallying cry after 9-11. With the passing of years, we have forgotten how united we were after the attack.

Today, eight years later, it is a very different kind of day in America, New York City and here at Orange Beach where I am writing. Reliving the events of that day brought me to tears and anger. No matter how painful it is to watch, it is infinitely more painful for those who lived, family members and the survivors of soldiers who have since died trying to protect us from another attack on our freedom.

As a nation united under God, it is our patriotic duty to never forget precisely how we felt on the day our innocence died.

Cousins on Clark Hill during the innocent years: Kevin Gooch, Frank Clark, Mark Clark, Kim Gooch, me, Randy Gooch, Marilyn, Phyllis and Linda Boutwell.

Karen Clark Rasberry

FAREWELL TO THE YEARS OF AUGHT

Just when I was getting accustomed to this decade and the use of aughts to designate the year, Father Time slipped in and pulled this decade right out from under me. It's astounding to think that we are about to enter the year 2010, when it seems that just a few months ago we were all uneasy about entering the new millennium. When I was a kid, the year 2010 seemed so far into the future that I could only imagine it as science fiction where everyone would be flying around in individual spacecrafts like the Jetsons. We are not quite there yet, but the advances in technology over the last ten years have put science fiction at our fingertips. There were, of course, huge political and social upheavals that rocked our nation in the past decade. And, there were those personal life-changing events that we knew were coming and tried to forget until they slapped us in the face.

a southernmost journey

We woke up one morning and stared fifty square in the face. Our children left the nest. Our parents left this world. And, sometimes we didn't recognize that person looking back at us in the mirror. Through it all, we persevered and looked forward with optimism to what the next year might bring.

Here's a look at a few of the things, for better or worse, that have changed our lives since the beginning of the millennium.

AIRPORTS: Remember when you didn't have to practically take all your clothes off before boarding a plane? Remember when you could bring a bottled drink or a fingernail file onboard? September 11, 2001, changed all that.

AARP cards...for boomers! I currently refuse to renew mine.

BLACKBERRIES: Introduced in 2002, the smart phone is an absolute essential for everyone, from pre-teens to CEOs.

BLOGS: They blog, you blog, he blogs...How did we spend our time before blogging?

CAMERAS: Remember those trips to get film developed? Nope? Even your grandmother has a digital camera and is probably e-mailing you Christmas photos right now.

CELL PHONES: More than 85% of the population in the U.S. has cell phones stuck to their heads. Landlines at home are becoming redundant. As a bonus, they've made cheating on a spouse very difficult... just ask Tiger Woods.

CROCS: You either love or hate these plastic fashion disasters. Personally, I wouldn't be caught dead at a tacky party in them, but First Lady Michelle Obama wore them on vacation in 2009. She knows better than that.

DANCING: Dancing never went out of style, but televised dancing contests became America's newest water cooler topic of conversation.

FACEBOOK: This time-sucking obsession for more than 300 million users poses a whole new social etiquette question. Who to friend on Facebook?

GPS: These replacements for road maps make it hard to get lost anymore, unless you enter the wrong address.

GREEN: It used to simply be a color, but now it is where everybody is going.

IPODS: It's hard to believe this portable media player was first launched in 2001, and has since become an icon of the digital age.

NETFLIX: Instead of you going to the movies, the movies come to you. Wish I had thought of that.

ORGANIC: Americans are such suckers. We will pay more for something if we think it's healthy, trendy or will promote our quest to go "green." How do we really know if a food is organic and not radioactive or something?

RETIREMENT: Thanks to the stock market crash, the word should probably be omitted from Webster's Dictionary.

STARBUCKS: At $4.00 for a gourmet cup-o-Joe that you could make at home for pennies, no wonder they could afford to build one on every corner in America.

TEXTING: LOL. OMG u r so fun e!

TWITTER: As long as you can say it in 140 characters or

less, you can tweet, retweet and keep twack of your fellow tweeters until your thumbs get cwamped.

UGGS: The fur-lined snow boots were everywhere. From Miami to L.A., the fashionable even wore them with shorts in the summer. Purchasing them is quite an investment, but your tootsies feel like they died and went to Heaven.

WIKIPEDIA: A Godsend to lazy students everywhere. If only we had had this back in our book report days.

YOUTUBE: Let's end this list and go kill some time watching videos. Thanks to this video-sharing site, everyone—including you—can be a star.

I hope all of you readers of the ReView have enjoyed my columns over the past year. It has been a privilege and a challenge to bare my soul and chronicle this mundane life of mine. If the Lord is willing, we are all on due course to enter a new decade at 12:00 tonight. It is my sincere wish that all of you have a year of prosperity and will see all of your hopes and dreams come to pass in 2010.

2011...2012...2013...2014...2015... Just practicing!

Karen Clark Rasberry

SAYING GOODBYE TO AN OLD FRIEND

Last Tuesday when my cell phone rang at 7:30 A.M., the number of a fellow realtor popped up. My instincts told me she was bearing the sad news we knew was imminent. Tuesday morning the Laurel Board of Realtors lost a very dear member of its family. Personally, I lost one of the best friends I've ever had.

      Charles D. Bates was my friend and mentor for half of my life. It seems like yesterday that I walked into his office on 15th Avenue in response to an ad he had placed in the paper. The year was 1982, and mortgage interest rates were in the teens. The oil boom in Jones County was waning and other industries weren't exactly scrambling to locate in Laurel. Nevertheless, Charles was optimistic about the future of real estate and the growth of Jones County. He agreed to be my sponsoring broker if I would take all the required classes and exams. In return, I promised to give it my best shot when others were leaving the profession in droves.

During the years that he was my broker, we never exchanged a cross word. That is remarkable, considering the pressure cooker nature of the real estate business. When Charles had a contract in the works, I always knew by the way he would come tearing into the office with his face all flushed and that preoccupied taking-care-of-business look in his eyes. Real estate wasn't simply his profession; it was who he was and what he did for fun and excitement. Hobbies didn't interest him because he preferred being out and about in the public where he could "stir" up something. He told me repeatedly, "Razz, you gotta' get out there and stir up business because it's not going to just fall in your lap." In recent years when I'd get lucky and sell a house or two, he would scold me, "Razz, I ought to kick your hiney for not doing that when you worked for me."

Charles and I didn't talk often enough after we became affiliated with different firms, but when we did we could cover a lot of territory in a matter of minutes. Because we each had a son, he always wanted to know how that "boy" of mine was doing. That invariably opened the door for him to brag about Jimmie Sue, Richard, Ginny and his grand young 'uns. Charles was passionate about real estate, but he was doubly passionate about his family. His every ambition was fueled by his desire to provide a good life for the family he loved so much.

After wrestling with the idea of retiring, he finally took the plunge about a year ago. He called me shortly after that, and the excitement in his voice was uplifting. "Hey, Raz! I bought a pontoon boat for the grand kids, and I need to know a good place to put it in the water at Orange Beach."

He went on and on about how life is too short not to enjoy it and that he fully intended to do so with his wife and family. During a month-long stay at the beach he discovered the joys of surf fishing and was aspiring to become a beach bum. He had finally arrived at the place he had worked so hard to be.

A few short months ago, I heard the news that Charles wasn't doing well. Something was terribly wrong, and his doctors couldn't diagnose the problem. Desperate for answers, Jimmie Sue took him to Cleveland Clinic in Ohio. The diagnosis was an extremely rare, always fatal brain disease. Creutzfeldt-Jakob Disease is the human form of Mad Cow Disease and is diagnosed in only 1 out of every 1 million patients annually. Charles' case was diagnosed as sporadic—possibly inherited but definitely not contagious or caused from eating infected beef.

Impossible odds. Charles was supposed to become one of those sprightly octogenarians that smile and nod at passersby on early morning beach walks.

My final goodbye was only a few days before he passed away. Although the disease had made his mind cloudy and his speech garbled, he managed to greet me with one last "Hey, Raz!" that I will keep near my heart for the rest of my life.

God puts different people in our lives for various reasons. It took me twenty-six years to understand why Charles Bates was a part of mine. He tried to teach me that success wasn't going to fall out of the sky into my lap. His death taught me that even those who deserve it the most aren't guaranteed a long, happy retirement. His passing also taught me that if you have a friend whose absence would leave a huge void in your life if he were gone; tell him so, before it's too late.

Dolly Parton and Charles D. Bates. He was my mentor and great friend for over 25 years.

Karen Clark Rasberry

A LETTER FROM "DUBYA" TO BARACK

Whether you loved or hated George W. Bush, you have to admit that his wild-west persona and well-intentioned bungling of the English language have provided us with much entertainment over the last eight years. His misstatements, pronunciations, malapropisms and hilarious misplacement of participles have come to be known as "Bushisms." With his eloquent speaking ability, silky, untangled words and GQish stage presence, president-elect Barack Obama appears to be the polar opposite of poor old, born-with-a-silver-foot-in-his-mouth George "Dubyah" Bush.

With excitement building and the inauguration of our new president only a few days away, I started thinking about what kind of advice Dubyah would give the incoming president. I imagined it in the form of a letter composed entirely of Bushisms left in the new commander in chief's desk in the Oval Office:

a southernmost journey

January 19, 2009

Dear Barack,

By the time you read this I will be down in Texas partying with my base—the "haves" and the "have mores." I'm looking forward to a good night's sleep on the soil of a friend. I'll be long gone before some smart person ever figures out what happened inside the Oval Office. I offer you my most heartwarming congratulations on being elected the first black president. It's very interesting when you think about it, the slaves who left Africa to go to America, because of their steadfast and their religion and their belief in freedom, helped change America. Whether they be Christian, Jew or Muslim, or Hindu, people have heard the universal call to love a neighbor just like they'd like to be called themselves.

We're here for a substanative talk on a lot of issues. I just want you to know that when we talk about war, we're really talking about peace. I think war is a dangerous place. Security is the essential roadblock to achieving the road map to peace. Our enemies are innovative and resourceful, and so are we. They never stop thinking about new ways to harm our country and our people, and neither do we. They will not hold America blackmail. We cannot let terrorists hold this nation hostile or hold our allies hostile. With strategery and principle, you can get the job done.

I would also like to offer a little advice on the economy. If terriers and bariffs are torn down this economy will grow. It's very important for folks to understand that when there's more trade, there's more commerce. The vast majority of our imports come from outside the country. I am very optimistic about our position in the world and about its influence on the United States. We're concerned about the short-term *economic news, but long-term, I'm optimistic. Dick Cheney and I did not want this nation to be in a recession. We wanted anybody who could find work to be able to find work. I understand small business growth. I was one. You hear what I'm saying, don't you— Obama-rama?*

One more problem our country faces is energy, the environment and abortion. If we don't succeed, we run the risk of failure. We need an energy bill that encourages consumption. Natural gas is hemispheric. I like to call it hemispheric in nature because it is a product that we can find in our neighborhoods. Hydrogen power will dramatically reduce greenhouse gas admissions. It isn't pollution that's harming the environment. It's the impurities in our air and water that are doing it.

It's important for us to explain to our nation that life is important. It's not only life of babies, but it's life of children living in, you know, the dark dungeons of the internet. My pro-life position is I believe there's life. It's not necessarily based in religion. I think there's a life there, therefore the notion of life, liberty, and pursuit of happiness.

Barack-o-buddy, you also can't misunderestimate the importance of education in America. Rarely is the questioned asked: Is our children learning? You teach a child to read, and he or her will be able to pass a literacy test. We are going to have the best-educated American people in the world. To those like you who received honors, awards and distinctions, I say well done. And to the C students, I say: They too, can be President of the United States.

And in closing, I think we agree the past is over. Our nation must come together to unite. There may be some tough times here in America. But this country has gone through tough times before, and we're going to do it again.

a southernmost journey

Finally, remember, public speaking is very easy. Always be ready for any unforeseen event that may or may not occur. The future will be better tomorrow. Most importantly, if you don't stand for anything, you don't stand for anything. Good luck.
And, may God bless America.
   Sincerestly yours, George

Just for the record, I liked him. A lot.

Karen Clark Rasberry

I HOPE YOU DANCE

This short trip through life is full of twists and turns, heartaches and absolute joy, rejection and acceptance, places and things that influence who we are and the different paths we take. It has taken me most of my life, and I might not have fully recognized this truth until a few days ago, but it is the people we love and love us in return, that make our journey worth taking.

This revelation came to me last Saturday while impatiently sitting in a traffic jam a few miles east of the tunnel in Mobile. Surrounded by thousands of cars full of people I didn't love and who most certainly didn't love me, I felt totally alone even though I was floating in a mass of humanity. I will spare you the details of a horrible week full of broken cars and computers and of real estate transactions gone down the drain, for they were just minor bumps in this road I'm traveling. The long wait on that short leg of my journey was spent in reflection and prayer for a kind and gentle man whose journey on Earth has ended.

Jerry Thurman came into my life about eight years ago when I re-entered the real estate business. In hindsight, I realize that it was not coincidence that landed us together. I'm slightly hesitant to say it was divine intervention, but I do believe that God puts people on the same path with us for a variety of reasons. It's part of the classroom of life where we can grow and learn by interacting with different people. Some are difficult to read, hard to comprehend and you lose interest in the subject. Although you may be wiser, you are no kinder or gentler for having known them. Others, who are few and far between, are a book you can't put down, who invite you into their lives, divide your burdens when you are in a valley and multiple your joys when you are on the mountaintop. Jerry H. Thurman, Sr. was such a man.

In the seven years I knew him, he never got flustered or angry over anything when he was in my presence. Real estate is a profession that often makes you feel as if you are in a pressure cooker. There were incidents that happened in the course of work that frequently made my valve blow, but Jerry always seemed to be on simmer, no matter how hot the fire underneath him got.

Over the years, we theoretically solved many of the world's problems in lengthy, informal front office meetings. We weathered many storms together, from the war in Iraq to Hurricane Katrina to the stock market crash. Of course we all were affected in one way or another, but through it all Jerry was a pillar in the wind, strong and unwavering in his faith that God was still in control.

Jerry was a mess. That's what we people in the South call someone who's always got a joke or a prank up his sleeve or is hilariously quick with the tongue. Jerry was a teller of corny jokes and old adages, interjecting them into Monday morning meetings with the perfect timing of a comedic sidekick. One morning he was telling us about a listing he was soon to acquire. In an attempt to describe the less than desirable property diplomatically, he chuckled a little and said, "Well, it's kind of like a bull a man tried to sell me one time years ago...it's old, but it's little." We laughed until we cried.

He was a shade-tree magician who could make quarters and his own thumb disappear before your very eyes—tricks that I loved to see as much as his grandchildren did. He was a firm believer in old wive's tales and a purveyor of home remedies, claiming my irritable intestines could be cured with a daily shot of hot sauce and a tablespoon of vinegar.

When my daddy passed away, he became the only father figure in my life who could make things all better with a hug. When my mother passed away, he called me, and in a voice that was obviously choking back tears, said he understood exactly what I was going through.

We shared a fondness for country music and often discussed newly released songs on the radio. He boasted on many occasions that in his younger years, he was often mistaken for Conway Twitty in looks and voice. Then to prove the likeness, he would shift his voice into baritone gear and croon, "Hello...darlin.'" How poignant and uplifting it was when I heard one of his favorite songs by Lee Ann Womack only a few minutes after he had passed away. From his new home in Heaven, I believe he had the radio play it for me and all the loved ones he left behind:

"*I hope you never lose your sense of wonder, get your fill to eat and always feel that hunger. May you never take one single breath for granted. God forbid love should ever leave you empty-handed. I hope you still feel small when you stand beside the ocean. When one door closes I hope another door opens. Promise me that you will give faith a fighting chance. And when you get the chance to sit it out or dance....I hope you dance.*"

Jerry H. Thurman, one of the kindest, most gentle men I've ever known.

Karen Clark Rasberry

HAPPY BIRTHDAY ELVIS

You faithful readers of the ReView know me well enough by now to know that there was no way I was going to let January 8th pass without fanfare. Although Elvis has been absent for his past 32 birthdays, that minor technicality is not going to stop me from remembering this very important milestone in his life. I'm sure you are all thinking that I'm one of those deranged fans whose walls are adorned with velvet paintings of him or that I have erected a shrine in my house where I keep candles burning around the clock. Or, that I own all of his music and keep it playing 24/7—365 days a year. None of that is the case, except I once painted a ceramic bust of him and displayed it on my mantle back in the late '70s. The fact that I have an authentic copy of his 1977 Tennessee driver's license and last will and testament stored in a safe deposit box is inconsequential because every Mississippian of a certain age owns those items. Don't they?

a southernmost journey

Thousands, even millions of words have been written about Elvis, and there is really nothing new to say except that he would have been 75 years old on January 8 if he had not accidentally killed himself with drugs. Nobody is perfect, so it would really humor me if you would please allow me to add a few more.

August 16, 1977, marked the passing of a legend and was the most somber of days for me and my sisters, Phyllis and Marilyn. Over the years I have tried to pinpoint exactly what it was that we felt we had lost. At age 42, his was a life interrupted when he still had so many more songs to sing, so many more hearts to break, so many more sappy movies to make. We were not done with him yet. And, we knew that for the rest of our lives no one would ever move us like he did. We just assumed that we would grow old along with him. Ironically, it is we who have grown older while Elvis has remained timeless.

There was a time when I still held out hope that his death was an elaborate hoax perpetrated by his inner circle so that he could live a normal life. I even fantasized about how he would return. It would have created the biggest media frenzy in history—-more sensational than the '68 Comeback times 10,000. With his concert version of *Burning Love* blaring on a loudspeaker, the Memphis Mafia would deliver him in a pink Cadillac right onto the front steps of Graceland. A fine, slender '60s Elvis but wearing a cape and sunglasses like the bloated '70s Elvis would slowly emerge from the back seat. Those stunned tourists who had not fainted from the shock of seeing him alive, would wait for him to speak. Humbly, apologetically and still with that delicious drawl, he would say, "Thank you. Thank you very much." He would have the souvenir shops torn down and order all the tacky wares to be burnt in a bonfire. Priscilla would hand over the keys to Graceland where he would live peacefully to a ripe old age. Little old silver-haired ladies all across America would escape from nursing homes and spryly make their way toward Memphis.

If Elvis were still alive...I am tortured by imaginings of where he would be now. Would his vanity have made him a recluse in the twilight of his fame? How would the world react today if he had merely suffered a timely death from old age? Would he still be performing in Vegas, or at a dinner theatre in Pigeon Forge? In the pathetic fashion of Wayne Newton or Burt Reynolds, would plastic surgery have left his face with a constant expression of waxy astonishment, or would he have let it droop forlornly like an old hound dog? Would we have been repulsed at the sight of a geriatric rock star in a jumpsuit struggling to swivel his titanium hips. Would he have had more #1 hits or won an Academy Award or had more children— someone to fill his blue suede shoes? In a few years, when those of us who loved him are also long gone, will they roll up the shag carpet in the Jungle Room due to a lack of interest? After all the numbers and charts are analyzed, will he still be the eternal King of Rock and Roll? It is all of the what-might-have-beens of a life interrupted that still haunt me so many years later.

All I know is this. A star that bright, burning so furiously, was never meant to burn for long. All of we who followed it and were blinded by it, and those who discovered it after it burned out, are convinced that Elvis was a once-in-a-millennium event.

Happy birthday Elvis! May you have 925 more.

a southernmost journey

me and Phil at Graceland paying tribute to
the king of rock n' roll — 1978.
(when I hoped Elvis was still alive)

Karen Clark Rasberry

COUNTRY ROADS TOOK HIM HOME

I have discovered that it is the friendships with people who knew you way back before you became who you are now are the most enduring ones. It's hard to impress those old friends because they witnessed your most ungraceful and embarrassing moments. They laughed at you until their sides hurt, and if you see them today, they will still laugh because they earned the right to do so. After all, they traveled shoulder to shoulder down those formative roads with you. They remember when you wore granny beads around your neck and no shoes on your feet. They know what color your hair should be and that you didn't always brush your teeth or take a bath when you were supposed to. They know where and when you received some of your early scars—the visible and the not so visible ones. When I think of this variety of endearing friendship, I think of the Lowerys.

Unless you were a barefoot country kid who lived so far out in the sticks that it took a little bit longer for the sun to set, this column might not resonate with you. For lack of a better description, we were a gang of free-range, country kids who didn't know or really care what other kids all over America were doing. Those other kids might have been catching waves in California, but we were catching tadpoles in a jar down at Bogue Homa Creek. While some kids were learning to saddle and properly handle horses, we were riding bareback through the woods on runaway mares. I have the scars to prove it.

The Lowerys were a loving, loud and jovial family who lived directly up the road from me in the direction of the Wayne County line. By bicycle, it took me no longer than a minute to reach the not-so-safe haven of their front yard. There were nine children in their family and four in mine. For every one of us Clark girls, there were at least two Lowerys of approximately the same age. My comrades and partners in childhood misadventures were Cammie (Sumrall), Robbie, Jonah T., and a menagerie of our cousins, nieces and nephews who enjoyed the free-range life.

We were the reverse of today's latchkey kids. You would never catch us inside watching T.V. during daylight hours. We actually played outside all day long without adult supervision and nobody was concerned that we would not turn up at suppertime. We never played video games, but we did play Tarzan on the vines in the holler behind their house. We drank water straight from a garden hose or cranked it out of a well and drank warm squirts of milk straight from a cow's teat. And we never caught any disease that couldn't be fixed with a strong dose of Milk of Magnesia. To get high, we climbed trees. And we fell out of those trees. Hard. For thrills we rode bikes down steep hills without hands or helmets. Chains came off. Brakes failed. As a result, we left a lot of flesh and blood on those perilous gravel roads. We rode in cars without seat belts and in the bed of pick-up trucks and never for one second considered that it might kill us. We played games with sharp sticks, ran with scissors, and threw heavy objects at each other as if they were as harmless as marshmallows. Although we were warned repeatedly that it would happen, we did not put out very many eyes. We ate corn straight from the stalk, green plums from the tree, over-ripe persimmons off the ground, and an occasional mud pie with worms. And the worms did not live in us forever.

We actually survived childhood without any hospitalizations, lawsuits or serious repercussions. As far as I know, none of us had any issues that hindered us from becoming productive adults.

We grew up. Times changed. The world became an unsafe place for children to roam free. We lost touch, but the bonds of a shared youth endured.

Last Sunday, they buried Jonah T. Lowery, a giant of a man with a heart to match, in the cemetery beside the road that we traversed countless times. Although his death was untimely, heartbreaking, and surreal in a way, I kept thinking that he would be pleased to be buried in the heart of our old stomping grounds on such a picture-perfect, almost spring day. Those country roads took him home one last time.

a southernmost journey

Jonah T. Lowery, Northeast Jones High School, class of 1973. A childhood friend who will be greatly missed by all those who knew him.

Karen Clark Rasberry

SALUTE TO A MARINE

You all know the way your heart skips a beat when a loved one calls at an odd hour of the day. When my sister's number showed up on my caller I.D. early this morning, instinct told me she was bearing bad news even before I heard her shaky voice on the other end. Everyone has had those moments when you don't want to answer, but you know you have to. I just closed my eyes, took a deep breath and said a prayer that whatever news Phyllis had wasn't going to be of the worst kind.

Our loving sister Marilyn, the kindest most gentle soul on Earth, found her husband dead this morning of a heart attack. Their marriage, the second for both of them, was like a broken-in pair of old boots, comfortable and warm. They found true love back in 1981 at a time when both of them really needed the companionship and security of a life partner. Many complicated circumstances caused their first marriage to dissolve. Then, a few years ago, they realized that life was too short to be alone and that the affection they had for each other had never really waned. I was their only attendant at the first wedding in 1981 and witnessed them take their vows again just two years ago.

Bob Maddox was a good man who loved my sister in his own special ways. He called her pet names like "Poochie" and "Babe." Although he was highly opinionated and headstrong, the result of being in the Marine Corps for several years, we learned to accept that he was going to give us instructions in life every time we were in his presence. My daughter spent a lot of time with him and MaeMae as a child, and I am positive that their influence helped to make her a successful and creative adult.

Bob is survived by four beautiful daughters and a handsome son, who is a Marine serving his third tour of duty in the war on terrorism. He was extremely proud of all of his children and grandchildren, but he lived for the day he could see his son again. The saddest part to me is that his son, at the expense of our freedom, had not seen his ailing father in eight months. Now, he never will. May God speed his journey home from Afghanistan for the final goodbye.

For the first time in her life, Marilyn will have no one to take care of, but she is a trooper and will survive this loss. Uncle Bob, we will miss your advice, your sense of humor and your heart-warming "ah-huh-huh-huh" laughter that always filled any room you entered.

Robert Maddox was a patriot to the core and was extremely proud of his service to his country as a Marine. This poem by John Wear was read at his eulogy as a tribute to him and all Marines who have served our country:

Karen Clark Rasberry

In a crowd you're bound to spot him,
He's standing so very tall
Not too much impresses him;
He's seen and done it all.
His hair is short, his eyes are sharp,
But his smile's a little blue.
It's the only indication
Of the hell that he's gone through.
He belongs to a sacred brotherhood,
Always Faithful 'til the end.
He has walked right into battle
And walked back out again.
Many people think him foolish
For having no regrets
About having lived through many times
Others would forget.
He's the first to go and last to know,
But never questions why,
On whether it is right or wrong,
But only do or die.
He walks a path most won't take
And has lost much along the way,
But he thinks a lot of freedom,
It's a small price to pay.
Yes, he has chosen to live a life
Off the beaten track,
Knowing well each time he's called,

a southernmost journey

He might not make it back.
So, next time you see a Devil Dog
Standing proud and true,
Be grateful for all he's given;
He's given it for you.
Don't go up and ask him
What's it's like to be in war;
Just thank God that it's your country
He's always fighting for.
And thank him too for all the hell
He's seen in that shade of green,
Thank him for having the guts
To be a United States Marine.

A farmer and a future Marine Bob and Wesley Maddox (1983).

Karen Clark Rasberry

A WORTHWHILE LIFE

My daughter, sisters, favorite aunt and I have been on a fervent trip down memory lane the past couple of weeks. Although we are always reminiscing about this, that and the other, we embarked on this latest voyage with great urgency upon realizing that it's past time to get serious about collecting pictures for my next book, *A Southernmost Journey*. Many of the kind people who read my last book commented that they would like to see more pictures in the next one. It's true that pictures make the words come to life when you see with your very own eyes who or what you are reading about. Of course, autobiographies are typically written by famous or extraordinary people who have made some contribution to history or mankind. I am as far from being famous or extraordinary as the North Pole is from Australia. Most of the columns I write for *The ReView* are inspired by events that occur in the course of my everyday life. I'm positive you could have written them much more skillfully about your own life if you were willing to embarrass yourself in public. It is my hope that they resonate with you because we have all traveled down the same roads and walked parallel paths on our journey through life.

While pouring over tattered photo album after album and digging through musty shoe boxes of family snapshots, Aunt Becky re-discovered a letter written by my PaPa Clark about two weeks after his adored wife passed away from cancer. She was sixty-nine years old and I had just turned ten when she lost her battle with cancer. It was my first experience with losing someone whom I wanted to live forever. The finality of her death didn't really sink in until much later as I reached different milestones in my life. She didn't get to see me bloom into a young woman, graduate or get married; and she never had the pleasure of spoiling her great-grandchildren in the same fashion she did her grandchildren. Through all the significant events of my life and on other days when I just needed a hug, there was always a longing in my heart and an unoccupied seat where she might have sat cheering me on

As you will understand, when you read the typed translation of the letter that was so eloquently written by my grandfather, tears flowed and noses blew. I could just imagine him there in the faint light of his living room, reminded of hours they spent together with every chime of the mantle clock, a notebook in his lap, his pipe resting in an ashtray, pining for his wife of fifty years, and not knowing that he would count the chimes of the clock alone for the next seventeen years. Although it wreaks havoc on women's mascara and prompts men to claim they've just got a little something in their eye, people deserve a good cry every now and then to set their souls right. My grandfather's words were so poignant and relative to our shared journey through life, that I felt the need to let you read them too:

Monday — Nov 9, 1965

> While here alone tonight I guess I'd better write this epistle about the main thing in my life. Anyone who knew us knows that main thing was my wife. From a lovely bride to an old lovely lady, she always did her job taking care of all her family—guided by love and the laws of God.
>
> She has been a sweetheart, wife and mother, a good neighbor and a true friend. I could keep on with her virtues, but the list would never end.
>
> We never had much money but we have had a wonderful life. The way I see it now, all that is needed is give and taking by the husband and wife.
>
> Close to 50 years we have been married—raised our family of three. We have had many, many blessings. No one really needs much more in this hour of grief and old age. I must say I am really thankful for a wondrous worthwhile life and I do from the depths of my heart thank you God for guidance and for such a wonderful life and also for such a wondrous, loving worthwhile wife.
>
> — H.G. Clark

The dictionary defines worthwhile as valuable, useful, meaningful, sensible and advisable. Of course, the antonym of worthwhile is worthless. The world has no more room for worthlessness. So now, I am deeply inspired by my grandfather's epistle to my grandmother. It should not be our ambition to live a meaningless life full of fame and fortune, but to live one that is simply, wondrously worthwhile.

My sisters Charlotte and Marilyn with my grandparents, Herman G. & Ola Sims Clark. (1951)

The Clark ancestral home. 1909-2009. It will stand forever in my memory.

A HOUSE PAINTED WHITE

When remembrances of the old house visit me, they are most often on the wings of a rope swing suspended from a gnarled oak tree in the back yard. I've discovered that it mainly depends on the season or the time of year. Around the holidays, I'm often transported to its living room floor spellbound by a scrawny, cedar Christmas tree that I helped my grandfather find in the woods. When summer comes around, my head is buried up to my ears in a huge watermelon slice with the juice dripping all the way to my elbows. In spring, I'm playing underneath the fragrant umbrella of a Magnolia tree in full bloom. Or, I'm running from bumblebees that buzz and float along the wisteria vines that smother the yard fence. In the coolness of fall, I'm diving into piles of leaves that have been raked up for burning.

For exactly one hundred years, the big, white house was a fortress perched on the crest of Clark Hill. Although the past few years have seen time and the elements take its toll on the old home place, it was once a testament to the pioneer spirit of the people who migrated to the Piney Woods of South Mississippi in the 19th Century.

My great-great grandfather, George Washington Clark, Sr. was born in South Carolina in 1826 and migrated to Wayne County sometime during the mid-nineteenth century. At the same time, on another branch of my family tree, Nancy Fountain Green, the widow of Confederate veteran George Green, moved to Eucutta from Burnt Corn, Alabama, because she had heard of a doctor who might be able to cure her breast cancer. George W. Clark, Jr. married her daughter, Mattie Green. Together, they staked out a tract of land in the nearby northeast corner of Jones County and gave birth to a branch of the family tree that includes me.

In 1909, when my grandfather, Herman G. Clark, was fourteen, his parents built a stately home beside the red, dirt road that runs from Sandersville to Eucutta, Mississippi. When my great-grandparents passed away, Herman and his wife Ola Sims Clark became the owners of the painted white house.

My earliest recollections of the house are now slipping from my grasp, but I have tried to keep them alive by making regular pilgrimages to the place where my memories and roots run deep into the Mississippi soil. Although I once knew the exact number of steps it required to reach my grandparents' house, it was no more than a few dozen steps from my own back door to the shelter of their loving arms.

It's strange how the fragrances of the house have endured while other recollections involving sight and sounds have diminished with age. To this day, my childhood memories are infused with the smell of sweet potatoes baking in the oven, the mustiness of aging wood, and of soot in a cold summer fireplace. Covered with a tin roof, the house had a wide front porch embellished with Victorian spindles and held creaky rocking chairs where the old folks would visit while the kids ran in and out slamming two screened doors that led into the double parlors of the house. When thunderstorms rolled in from the south, we could smell them coming and we kids would seek refuge under the porch. It was a magical and calming noise that I would like to hear again someday before I leave this world. The front porch is where we lived publicly, but the back porch is where I could skip around freely in my panties and preen in the mirror beside the back kitchen door where three generations of Clark men once shaved.

The old house has been a shelter in the storm, a sanctuary in our hour of need and the cradle of our family's history. It and its inhabitants were witnesses to depression and war, prosperity and peace, joy and sadness. It has held beds for newlyweds and newborns, those who were just beginning to live, and those who were dying. It has opened its arms to returning soldiers and welcomed kinfolk and friends from near and far. Five generations of Clark ancestors called it home, beginning with my great-grandparents and ending with my sister, Marilyn and her son, Steve Harris. Steve spent his formative years in the house from the time he was five years old. I fear that he will not take this well on his next visit when he finds that only the chimney remains.

In the interim when Clarks didn't live in it, several families of tenants put down roots in our beloved domain. When I was in high school, my grandfather rented it to a family that included my new best friend. Thus began another memorable chapter of my life where the old, white house played a major role. If its walls could talk, it could tell of giggling teenaged girls, two peas in a pod who shared everything until the tearful day she moved away, never to be seen again. We were just dreamy-eyed girls who missed knowing the woman the other became.

Though we all own precious memories of the house, Marilyn is the one who spent the greatest number of her days there. By the time she called it home, most of its grandeur was gone. She spent her winters trying to keep it warm, battling frozen pipes and cold wind that whipped under the doors, down the chimneys and through the rattling windowpanes. On the coldest of nights, a glass of water left by the kitchen sink would be frozen solid come morning. Summers were a bit better when the wide porches caught a breeze and the tall ceilings kept the sultry air aloft. There was not a right angle in the house and the kitchen sloped off the back at a 45-degree angle. It gave me the feeling of being in the fun house at the fair—a little off balance and tipsy. Some doors had to be kicked and cussed to open and shut them, while others gaped open like barn doors in the wind. The faucets dripped perpetually and the water built up deltas of rust stains in the sinks. The breakers tripped with the slightest provocation. Consequently, she could not run the window unit in the living room and bake a cake at the same time.

My children, particularly my daughter, spent many contented hours there being spoiled and pampered at the hands of their aunt. As fifth generation Clarks, I'm so thankful that my children were bathed in the aura of their ancestral home.

Although I've tried to imagine the scene in my mind a hundred times, my heart cannot fathom how my grandmother withstood her emotions as she stood on that front porch and hugged her two sons, Ralph and Charlie Paul, goodbye when they went to serve in World War II. Nor can I imagine the joy she felt from her vantage point in the kitchen window when she saw her boys triumphantly rising up the hill in a cloud of dust on that red, dirt road.

It's heartbreaking to know that when I return, the old fortress will be gone. While the finality of it is almost like the death of a loved one, we all knew the day was coming when something would have to be done. It just wasn't financially feasible to try to restore it and much too painful to simply let the proud old house fall down with our history inside it.

It's very fitting that my sister is overseeing the demolition and trying to salvage what she can so each of us can preserve a piece of the past. If she, the one who has the most memories vested in it, has the courage to tear it down, then the rest of us must be brave enough to let it go. I keep telling myself it is just old boards and rusty tin and not flesh and blood, but it sure feels like it. It's just that the house is so much a part of the deep places of my heart. As surely as I inherited a furrowed brow from my daddy and the green in my eyes from my mother, the imperfections and desirable traits of the house run through my blood just the same. My southernmost journey through life began with the house. It is in my voice, my country-girl sensibilities, my character, and in the nostalgic words I write. Although I only lived in its shadow and have resided away from it for most of my life, my southern identity dwells in the cool shade of its trees and porches.

The contractor who is tearing it down declares the foundation is made of some of the finest virgin timber he's ever seen. Like the hardworking people who built it in 1909, it was made of some pretty strong stuff.

We Clarks could have told him that.

My daddy and nephew, Steve Harris, with his children Seth and Emily in front of the family homestead (2001).

Five generations of the descendants of George W. Clark Jr. and Mattie Green Clark (1984). Many have passed on, and many have since been born.

photo by McAlister Creative

Karen Clark Rasberry is a lifelong resident of Jones County and Laurel, Mississippi. Her work has been published nationally and she is a columnist for *The ReView* of Jones County. Her last book, *Travelers in Search of Vacancy*, was named best non-fiction in the South by the Independent Publisher Awards in 2010. Karen has been married for 36 years and has a grown son and daughter. This is her third book.

CPSIA information can be obtained
at www.ICGtesting.com
Printed in the USA
LVHW090747080122
708102LV00018B/204